BECOMING PERFECT

Let The Perfector Perfect His Work In You

A Guide for Spiritual Journey

BECOMING PERFECT

Let The Perfector Perfect His Work In You

by Sally Stokes Weiesnbach

BOLD TRUTH PUBLISHING

Christian Literature & Artwork

A BOLD TRUTH Publication

BECOMING PERFECT

ISBN 10: 0-9991469-1-2
ISBN 13: 978-0-9991469-1-0

FIRST EDITION

Sally Stokes Weiesnbach
Ark of Faith Foundation
PO Box 1412
Muskogee, Oklahoma 74402
www.arkoffaith.org
sally@arkoffaith.org

BOLD TRUTH PUBLISHING *(Christian Literature & Artwork)*
606 West 41st, Ste. 4
Sand Springs, Oklahoma 74063
www.BoldTruthPublishing.com
beirep@yahoo.com

The views expressed in this book are not necessarily those of the publisher.

Printed in the USA.
07 17   10 9 8 7 6 5 4 3 2

PERMISSIONS

PERMISSIONS

PERMISSIONS

CONTENTS

ACKNOWLEDGMENTS ....*i*

HOW TO USE THIS GUIDE ....*iii*

Week 1. **Father's Light** 1

Week 2. The Hebrew Word for Intercession 3

Week 3. **After the Meeting, What Next?** 6

Week 4. Being the Church Today 8

Week 5. **What is God Saying to You?** 13

Week 6. Show Me, Lord 16

Week 7. **In Fall Harvest Time** 19

Week 8. Walk In Love 21

Week 9. **Called to Follow Christ's Example** 27

Week 10. What Am I Learning? 29

Week 11. **Getting on with Perfecting and Maturing** 32

Week 12. A Perfect Day Requires Gospel-style Action 35

Week 13. **Do Not Restrain the Holy Spirit** 39

Week 14. Perfect Obedience to Father God 42

Week 15. **Hear, you deaf! ...and See, you blind!** 44

Week 16. God's Goal: Perfect Children 47

Week 17. **God Continues Making Perfect Children** 51

Week 18. So Let the Perfect Come 53

Week 19. **All the Way---No Halfway Stances** 55

Week 20. Enter His Presence 58

Week 21. **Perfect Unity** 63

Week 22. Spared the Shame of Defeat 66

Week 23. **Jesus, Remove Our Imperfections!** 68

Week 24. Do Everything Without Complaining or Arguing 71

Week 25. **Glory To The Righteous One** 75

Week 26. The Law of The Lord Is Perfect 77

Week 27. **Father Perfectly Instructs Me** 79

Week 28. May God Be With You In Everything You Do 81

Week 29. **The Perfection of Beauty** 86

Week 30. Perfect Love Drives Out All Fear 90

Week 31. **Look Closely Into the Perfect Law That Sets People Free** 92

Week 32. Perfect Security 94

Week 33. **Perfectly Safe** 99

CONTENTS

Week 34. Above All: Pray 101

Week 35. **Chosen to Be Holy and Without Fault** 104

Week 36. **Jesus, Perfector of Our Faith** 106

Week 37. **How Dependable His Words** 111

Week 38. Pure In Act and Thought 113

Week 39. They Are Faultless 115

Week 40. The Will of God is Good... Pleasing... Perfect 117

Week 41. **Wait For Holy Spirit Guidance** 122

Week 42. Blood of Christ---a Perfect Sacrifice to God 124

Week 43. **Yes, You Can Be A Perfect Man** 126

Week 44. Christ Loved The Church and Gave His Life For It 130

Week 45. **Let Us Go On Unto Perfection** 134

Week 46. Are We in Him? 136

Week 47. **Release His Anointing** 138

Week 48. Choose to Purify Ourselves and Be Completely Holy 141

Week 49. **Think of Us as Christ's Servants** 145

Week 50. We Pray You Will Become Perfect 147

Week 51. **The Son Who Has Been Made Perfect Forever** 150

Week 52. Just as Your Father in Heaven is Perfect 152

OVER ABUNDANCE
7 Additional Lessons from The Father 157

Number 1. Do We Have a Perfect Heart Toward Him? 157

Number 2. **Let Every Temptation Add to Perfection** 159

Number 3. Put on the Bond of Perfectness 162

Number 4. **That We May Grow Into the Fullness of Christ** 164

Number 5. Perfecting Holiness in the Fear of God 166

Number 6. **Be Holy** 168

Number 7. The Revelation of His Perfect Love Drives Out Fear ... 170

ACKNOWLEDGMENTS

First, I thank God, Jesus Christ and the Holy Spirit for putting this work in my path. I thank Mary, Jim and Emily Dum for encouragement, helpful contributions and typing of Ark of Faith, Foundation, Inc.'s newsletter. The production of that newsletter is where I realized that this would be a book. My gratitude also goes to the many volunteers, family, spiritual family, and friends who supported me with prayer, technical assistance and as partners in my spiritual walk. To my loving husband, Garry, I bless and thank you for much assistance with concordance research of Scriptures. This guide would not be available if not for Sharee Wells' editing. Finally, my thanks go to Bruce Nelson and Suzanne Karreman for constant encouragement and publishing assistance.

HOW TO USE THIS GUIDE

These days, it is commonly accepted that people can't be perfect because "We're only human," or "Jesus was the only perfect person," or some other excuse. Frankly, to me, these concepts come off as rationalizations to ease our guilt for two situations in which we find ourselves:

1) settling for being less than who God intended us to be, or

2) behaving like perfectionists where we or other humans set our own standards and try to live up to them and / or force everyone else to live up to them as well.

"But you are to be perfect, even as your Father in heaven is perfect." (**Matthew 5:48 NLT**) You see, according to Scripture, God wants us to become perfect. We have to become holy and perfect to be with Him in Heaven. He didn't expect us to make our own selves perfect, but told us that He would make us perfect as we strive to obey His commands. He provided us with Jesus as the example and, when Jesus was sacrificed to save our souls, God sent us the Holy Spirit to help us follow Jesus' example of how to do God's will in our lives.

This book is intended to assist your spiritual growth and life journey toward the perfection that God wants for you. The guide has evolved from my personal adventure and study of God's will and purpose to perfect me in my life. First, I had to get to know the Holy Spirit as the third person of the Trinity! It is the Spirit of God Who works within each of us to perfect us and make us holy. If we do not ask for His help, we won't get it! Second, we must pray to be perfect---not to be a perfectionist or religious zealot trying to perfect our own selves or live up to our man-made standards. Thirdly, we must receive the blessings and righteousness of Christ's grace---His finished work on the cross. This is the good news. It is finished. The forgiveness and grace of God are undeserved. They cannot be achieved, only received! Spending time alone with God daily will turn your disappointments and problems into highways when you accept His Word as directly spoken to you! So, I wrote down my experience to encourage your own.

I hope that you will use this guide in the same way that it was given:

1) Accept that going on this journey means that you must first accept the Holy Spirit as the third person of the Trinity---the counselor, the helper, the power that enables you

2) Schedule daily time to "meet" with God. Commit to spending this time with God every single day in order to practice meditating (thinking specifically) on these principles of how the Holy Spirit works in you.

HOW TO USE THIS GUIDE

3) Ponder and consider these lessons as they are set out---weekly. Studying and meditating on a lesson for a week or more helps you to understand it thoroughly.

4) Understand the structure of each lesson. The weekly journey begins with the Scripture on which the lesson is based, the lesson itself, a prayer, and then extra resources (from different translations of the Bible) for you to meditate on through the week and make notes on what the Holy Spirit reveals to you, personally.

5) Allow yourself to grow in intimacy with the Holy Spirit. You should end each "meeting" with God by asking the Holy Spirit to open your eyes, your ears, and your heart to know Him more clearly.

This is the way Father God used the Scripture to reveal to me His desire to perfect me by teaching me to let the Holy Spirit guide me through a life of following His Only Son's perfect example. I am now allowing The Perfector to make me into the Child of God I should be. I hope you will find your way to becoming perfected by studying the lessons I have learned and written in this guide.

⬛⬛⬛ ⬛ ⬛◀◆▶⬛ ⬛ ⬛⬛⬛

"Moses went up Mount Sinai, and a cloud covered it. The dazzling light of the Lord's presence came down on the mountain. To the Israelites, the light looked like a fire burning on top of the mountain…"
(Exodus 24:15-17 GNB)

Father's Light

◄ *WEEK 1* ►

Can we become so familiar with that idea that we miss the true essence of Father God? I must admit, I did just that. Yes, Jesus did say, *"…it is better that I go away… I will send the Helper … to you."* **(John 16:7 GNB)** Praise the Lord; this is true! Indeed, my life is and has been better. It's been moving forward since I asked (used my voice) for the Holy Spirit to come to help, lead, guide, and teach me of His truth! Thank You, Jesus!

Like Paul, I am still trying daily to give up my own understanding of His Words and the servanthood and reconciliation work He calls each of us to do. Jesus never did or said one thing that He had not seen the Father do or heard the Father say. Yes, in the beginning, Jesus and the Holy Spirit were there with Father God when He said, *"Let us make man in our image, after our likeness…"* **(Genesis 1:26 KJV)** Jesus was always with God---He was family. We were created to be family. We know Father God sent Jesus to reconcile us to Himself. God our Father gave His only Son that we might know His Spirit: the Spirit of God. The Father's desire is that each person might know Him, fellowship, and have intimate family relationship with Him.

Through Dutch Sheets' book, *Intercessory Prayer*, I found the greatest joy in asking our Father to *"send His lightning-like power to hit the mark"* **(Job 36:32 GNB)** for whatever I am praying about. Only our Father knows the beginning through the end. Jesus even stated, *"Only My Father knows the day of My return."* **(Matthew 24:35 GNB)** Only the Father knows A to Z.

We are to partner with God. Our part is to ask Him… beseech Him… humble ourselves (repent of our sin). *"Then will He hear from heaven and heal…"* **(II Chronicles 7:14 GNB)** He will heal our world, countries, cities and states, our families, workplaces, courts and prison systems, churches---every element of our societies. There is big need in every area of daily life. Is Heaven in your home, office, church, business or ministry? Jesus taught, *"pray like this: Our Father, who art in heaven, hallowed be Thy name... Thy kingdom come on earth as it is in heaven..."* **(Matthew 6:9-15 GNB)**

Is Heaven in your home? Have you asked? If we don't ask, knock, seek, we will not receive! It is not that God cannot give us Heaven without our asking, but rather it is because He gave us free will to choose. He tells us to ask. He wants us to choose to intentionally ask. He tells us that if two agree on earth it will be done, in Jesus' Name. All through the Bible, Scriptures say that God our Father has 'lightning-like power.' If we ask, He will use it on our behalf. We are told to be the light of the world. My light switch or candle or flashlight takes darkness from the room. But His lightning-like power flashes suddenly and lights up the whole sky! It can split a giant tree in two pieces.

Have you ever seen lightning hit a giant tree and split it right in two? Usually, there is fire. A friend discovered that, when lightning hits the tree, the fire starts underground. A group of us are studying this concept through God's Word. What have you covered up that needs the lightning power of God to hit the mark and burn it up from its base? Jealousy? Bitterness? Unforgiveness? Hatred? Rage? Something else? It must begin with us as individuals, but, as we partner with God and intercede for others, we will see and experience His greater power, in Jesus' Name. Then we must thank God! This is the sacrifice He requires: A grateful heart!

PRAYER

As it says in (Jeremiah 31:16-18 GNB) "...stop crying and wipe away your tears. All that you have done for your children will not go unrewarded; they will return from the enemy's land. There is hope for your future; your children will come back home..." I pray this to you, Lord. You have spoken it. I ask for You, Father God, to come with "lightning-like power to hit the mark and enable each of us **(verse 18)** *. . . to obey . . . to forgive. Father, bring us back; we are ready to return to You, our Lord God." Amen.*

MEDITATE ON THESE PASSAGES

Zechariah 9:14-15 (GNB) *"The Lord will appear above His people; He will shoot His arrows like lightning... the Lord Almighty will protect His people..."*

Colossians 1:13 (AMP) *"[The Father] has delivered us from the domain of darkness...and transferred us into the kingdom of the Son of His love."*

II Corinthians 5:18-19 (AMP) *"...Who... reconciled us to Himself through Christ . . . [God, personally present] in Christ...restoring... reconciling the world to... Himself."*

■ ■ ■   ■ ■◄◆►■ ■   ■ ■ ■

"But it was to us that God made His secret by means of His Spirit. The Spirit searches everything, even the hidden depths of God's purposes... We have not received this world's spirit; instead, we have received the Spirit sent by God, so that we may know all that God has given us."
(I Corinthians 2:10, 12 GNB)

The Hebrew Word for Intercession

◄ WEEK 2 ►

"Paga" is the Hebrew word for intercession and it means "to meet." Intercession is not primarily a prayer. Intercession is a meeting with God. Its purpose is to get His leading and determine His will for us since we only know in part, but He knows the total picture. This fellowship with Him is why we need to spend daily time with God.

Christ is The Intercessor! He is sitting at the right hand of God *"...he always lives to make intercession for them."* **(Hebrews 7:25 ESV)** Intercession brings together a person or persons in fellowship with God. The purpose of these meetings is to effect reconciliation with Our Father.

The first Adam met with God in a garden, Eden. Adam was tempted and gave in to Satan. The last Adam, Jesus, was tempted for the final time in a garden, Gethsemane, and He overcame it. Jesus travailed (toiled, struggled) in Gethsemane! Yes, Jesus labored, bore our pain, and brought forth our forgiveness and reconciliation with Father God! He heard His Father and obeyed. He did this to bring forth a new family as was foretold for centuries through many prophets. Jesus shed His blood and bore pain to restore our acceptance. Christ met the Father to create a meeting between God and humankind.

3

BECOMING PERFECT

"...loving-kindness and truth have met together; righteousness and peace have kissed each other." **(Psalms 85:10 AMP)** Sin cannot be excused or justified. It must be judged and repented and we must be washed with His blood to be made clean. Yes, *"All of this is from God, who reconciled us to himself through Christ and gave us the ministry of reconciliation..."* **(II Corinthians 5:18-19 NIV)** Through our prayerful intercession, we too, release the fruit of what Jesus Christ accomplished. We are His bride The Church and we are given the ministry of reconciliation in the world. The purpose of such prayer is to create meetings between God and man.

If we are compassionately willing, we can ask the Father to meet with someone needing Christ and the Helper, the Holy Spirit. If we don't ask for the meeting with Father God and the unsaved, who will? There are so many sad, hopeless, diseased, and hurting people in today's world. Can we create more prayer gatherings so the Father can meet them at their individual points of need? *"Paga"*, the Hebrew word translated as "intercession", is sometimes a battlefield term. Intercession can be violent and hard work! Have you ever been at a meeting that became violently unpleasant?

For some time now, the Holy Spirit has led me to pray the last three verses of **Psalms 91** over family, friends and unsaved people. I am using the Good News Bible. Look for yourself in **verse 14.** Father God says, *"I will save those who love me and will protect those who acknowledge me as Lord."* How can we acknowledge Him as Lord if we've never met Him? There must be a meeting---a *paga*! Continue reading to **verse 15** to see what happens after the meeting, *"When they call to me, I will answer them; when they are in trouble, I will be with them; ...I will rescue them..."* Again, meeting, togetherness, being present with God brings *"honor... and reward... long life and safety... He will save..."* in Jesus' powerful Name! **(Psalms 91:10-16 GNB)**

Praise the Lord, we can pray together, hold prayer meetings and do our part! Our responsibility is to enforce victory, to meet the powers of darkness through Spiritual warfare. Through prayers of intercession, we meet the powers of darkness with God to bring about reconciliation. A meeting with God must take place with each of us to evoke change, heal wounds and meet individual need. I repeat: our responsibility is to enforce victory as we meet the powers of darkness through Spiritual warfare.

Jesus used a Greek word, *"luo"*, to describe what we (The Church) are to do. In **(Matthew 16:19 GNB)**, Jesus tells us, *"I will give you the keys of the kingdom of heaven; and* *whatever you shall bind on earth shall be bound in heaven, and whatever you shall loose on earth shall be loosed in heaven."* The word "loose" in this verse is *"luo".* Although Jesus fully defeats the devil on the cross, someone on earth must represent Him in that victory to enforce it!

PRAYER

Yes, Lord, through prayers of intercession, we meet the powers of darkness and enforce the victory You accomplished when You met those powers in Your intercession while on earth. You told us to go and do all we'd seen and heard You do. It doesn't matter whether we saw or heard it in Scriptures or in answered prayers in today's world! Jesus is the Way, the Truth and the Life. Through the Holy Spirit, let us be used in representing Jesus so lives may be changed today! Amen.

MEDITATE ON THESE PASSAGES

I Peter 3:18-19 (GNB) *"For Christ died for sins once, for all, a good man on behalf of sinners, in order to lead you to God. He was put to death physically, but made alive spiritually and in His spiritual existence He went and preached to the imprisoned spirits."*

I Peter 2:24 (GNB) *"Christ himself carried our sins in His body to the cross, so that we might die to sin and live for righteousness. It is by His wounds that you have been healed."*

Matthew 28:18-20 (GNB) *"Jesus drew near and said to them, 'I have been given all authority in heaven and on earth. Go then, to all peoples everywhere and make them My disciples: baptize them in the name of the Father, the Son, and the Holy Spirit, and teach them to obey everything I have commanded you. And I will be with you always, to the end of the age.'*

"If you remain in Me and My words remain in you,
then you will ask for anything you wish, and you shall have it."
(John 15:7 GNB)

After the Meeting, What Next?

◂ *WEEK 3* ▸

As intercessors, we go between an individual and the powers of darkness asking Father God to break the hold of Satan with the power of Christ. In the Name of Jesus, we can command Satan to loose (*"luo"*) his hold over a person and let him or her go. **(Matthew 16:19 GNB)** Remember Jesus tells us, *"I will give you the keys of the kingdom of heaven; and whatever you prohibit on earth will be prohibited in heaven, and what you permit on earth will be permitted in heaven."* We enforce the victory of the Cross when we do and speak, not just read or think, but actually, responsibly obey! Someone on earth must represent Jesus and speak His Name to intercede and loose the powers of light and bind the powers of darkness.

Jesus fully accomplished the task of breaking the authority of Satan and powers of darkness and told us to follow His example. We are to use the keys of His example to open doors and set captives free from satanic torment. This is not done by human beings. It is done only after discerning what and when the Holy Spirit and Father God want. The Holy Spirit can do this through us when we mention the Name of Jesus. So, there must be a meeting with God---either to reconcile with His blessings and promises or to meet satanic forces of opposition and enforce the victory that was won at Calvary.

The prayers of intercessors who understand and fully cooperate with God create meetings that bring change and create a new being with the *"mind of Christ"* **(I Corinthians 2:16 ESV)** and the loving heart of Christ. Jesus has qualified us to represent Him and has not given a spirit of timidity. No intimidation because we've been given the Spirit *"of power, and of love, and of a sound mind."* **(II Timothy 1:7 GNB)** We can step between the individual and the evil forces wanting to *"... steal, kill, and destroy..."* **(John 10:10 GNB)** to meet them in the Name of Jesus. Jesus did not just pray. He did a work and told us to *"go and do... likewise...:* **(Luke 10:37 KJV)** His work paved the way for us to do our part! Jesus, who knew no sin *"became sin in our behalf... that we may become the righteousness of God in him."* **(II Corinthians 5:21 NIV)** *"We must remain in Him; Remain connected to the vine and allow our Father... (to trim off... take away); and He cleanses and repeatedly prunes every branch that continues to bear fruit, to make it bear more and richer and more excellent fruit."* **(John 15:1-10 AMP)**

"At one time you were far away from God and were His enemies because of the evil things . . . you did and thought. But now, by means of the physical death of His Son, Father God has made you friends, in order to bring you holy, pure, and faultless into his presence". **(Colossians 1:21-22 GNB)** Paul became a servant and I did too. What about you?

"...I have been made a servant of the church by God, who gave me this task to perform for your good. It is the task of fully proclaiming His message..." **(Colossians 1:25-26 GNB)** My life is to intercede for others to meet, come to know and remain in Him. *"To get this done I toil and struggle, using the mighty strength which Christ supplies and which is at work in me."* **(Colossians 1:29 GNB)** Now read **(Colossians 1:24 GNB)**: *"And now I am happy about my sufferings for you, for by means of my physical sufferings I am helping to complete what still remains of Christ's sufferings on behalf of his body, the church."* You see that Paul says that there are still sufferings being completed for the sake of The Church. **(II Corinthians 1:11 AMP)** tells us to *"...cooperate, laboring and praying together for the deliverance, that the many [intercessors] may return and give thanks."*

It is a glorious, fun, exciting, and at times, painful labor. However, if we continue to be faithful in these things, our Father will receive all the glory! It is all so simple: Do the Word! Pray without ceasing! Intercede! Listen! Hear and obey! His Power will be manifested because we asked. We knocked and the door opened. This is what makes us able to serve.

PRAYER

In **(Job 36:15 GNB)** *the Scripture says, "God teaches people through suffering and uses distress to open their eyes." Father, we do not want needless suffering and we do want our eyes opened during these stressful times. I ask in Jesus' Name, Amen.*

MEDITATE ON THESE PASSAGES

John 15:4 (GNB) *"Remain united to me, and I will remain united to you. A branch can-*

not bear fruit by itself; it can do so only if it remains in the vine. In the same way you cannot bear fruit unless you remain in me."

John 15:1-6 (WEB) *"I am the true vine, and my FATHER is the farmer. Every branch in me that doesn't bear fruit, he takes away...he prunes, that it may bear more fruit...unless you remain in me...you can do nothing. If a man doesn't remain in me, he is thrown out as a branch ... withered... and they are burned."*

■■■　■　■◀▶■　■　■■■

"Phillip said to Jesus, 'Lord, show us the Father [cause us to see the Father – that is all we ask]; Then we shall be satisfied.' Jesus replied, 'Have I been with all of you for so long a time, and do you not recognize Me yet, Phillip? Anyone who has seen Me has seen the Father. How can you say then, show us the Father?'"
(John 14:8 AMP)

Being the Church Today

◀ WEEK 4 ▶

Jesus had spent a long time working with, being present with, teaching, loving, sharing and caring for His disciples... wanting, desiring and developing a close and intimate relationship with each of them. Was He saddened, hurt, angry that they still failed to understand... or that they even refused to truly know Him as the Christ of God?

They watched Him minister to people that others would cast aside. They appeared to have learned little... they had knowledge without intimacy. Even Satan had knowledge of Him! Are we only intellectually aware of who He is and what it means to be in ministry? Is it easier to do the work of God -- feeding the hungry, clothing the naked, praying for the sick, comforting the dying, visiting those in prison as we are instructed in **Matthew 25:35-36** (of any Bible) -- than to encourage intimacy with Father God? The works list goes on: caring for the orphan and widow, assembling at church, teaching the Word, being good stewards, decorating the church, preparing communion, visiting shut-ins, and more. Is it easier to do the work, perhaps working so hard for Jesus that we forget to work with Jesus? Jesus desires intimacy more than works. Once we know Him, truly know Him and the Holy Spirit, we'll be more obedient doers of the Word.

Truth: faith without works is dead. We know works don't get us to Heaven but that belief in Him (faith) is the only way. We must choose to stay connected, to *"remain united"* to the Vine Jesus. **(John 15:1-4 GNB)** Why? *"...so that"* each of us *"will be clean and bear more fruit... "a branch cannot bear fruit by itself; it can do so only if it remains in the vine."* Connection or "connected to" means "presence with". This means much more than head knowledge and works. In **(John 8:12 GNB)** Jesus states, *"I am the light of the world... whoever follows me will have the light of life and will never walk in darkness."* He was talking to the Pharisees, saying that religious practices and works prove nothing. Jesus went on to say, *"I testify on my own behalf, and the Father who sent me also testifies on my behalf... If you knew me, you would know my Father also..."* **(John 8:18-19 GNB)**

Getting to know God takes time, sharing, intimacy. Two are better than one; *"For if they fall, the one will lift up his fellow..."* **(Ecclesiastes 4:9 KJV)** *"...if two on earth agree..."* **(Matthew 18:19 KJV)** -- not acquiesce or just quietly accept, but, in harmony and one accord, truly come together in agreement -- it will be done in Jesus' Name. The will and purpose of God means the intent of heart, not just mental assent. Father God's heart is to have a holy family! This type of family is built in relationships that use agape love. The word *'agape'* (ah-GAH-peh) is Greek for "love: the highest form of love, charity" and "the love of God for man and of man for God".

Jesus gave His life so that we might be restored to the Father by His Holy Spirit. Jesus said, *"...I say only what the Father has instructed me to say... If you obey my teaching, you are really my disciples; you will know the truth, and the truth will set you free."* **(John 8:28-32 GNB)** He goes on to say, *"I talk about what my Father has shown me..."* He uses a teacher's kind of "Show and Tell", a presence, and goes on to add in **verse 38** *"...but you do what your father has told you."* Do you notice how the heavenly Father's talk and demonstrations differ from the earthly examples of Satan, the *"father of lies"*? Have you ever been deceived or lied to? No real, true relationship is built on lies and half-truths. There would be no trust.

It is my hope that each of us will *"ask... seek... knock"* **(Matthew 7:7 KJV)** and find the inner doors of our hearts opening to allow the Holy Spirit to reveal new desires from God's heart. I want that so we'll not only serve and work for Him but also enjoy a Spirit-filled, intimate relationship with Our Triune God. *"My friends, be careful that none of you have a heart so evil and unbelieving that you will turn away from the living God. Instead, in order that none of you be deceived by sin and become stubborn, you must help one another every day… For we are all partners with Christ if we hold firmly to the end the confidence we had in the beginning."* **(Hebrews 3:12 GNB)**

I received an email from one of my daughters. She forwarded this quote by Stephan Hoeller, in reference to a discussion we'd had on suffering in order to grow:

> "A pearl is a beautiful thing that is produced by an injured life. It is the tear that results from the injury of the oyster. The treasure of our being in this world is also produced by an injured life. If we had not been wounded, if we had not been injured, then we would not produce the pearl."

PRAYER

Perhaps you will join me in reading and praying Romans 8:28 *"We know that in all things God works for good for those who love Him and are called according to His purpose" and so we ask You, Father, for Your purpose in our lives, in Jesus' Name. Amen.*

MEDITATE ON THESE PASSAGES

John 9:31 (GNB) *"We know that God does not listen to sinners; he does listen to people who respect Him and do what He wants them to do."*

John 15:7-8 (GNB) *"If you remain in Me and My words remain in you, then you will ask for anything you wish, and you shall have it. My Father's glory is shown by your bearing much fruit; and in this way you become my disciples."*

John 15:10 (GNB) *"If you obey my commands, you will remain in my love, just as I have obeyed My Father's commands and remain in His love."*

NOTES: _____

_____
_____
_____
_____
_____
_____
_____
_____
_____
_____
_____
_____
_____
_____
_____
_____
_____
_____
_____
_____
_____
_____
_____
_____
_____
_____

DIRECTION: _____

_____
_____
_____
_____
_____
_____
_____
_____
_____
_____
_____

PROGRESS: _____

_____
_____
_____
_____
_____
_____
_____
_____
_____
_____
_____

■ ■ ■　■　■◄◆►■　■　■ ■ ■

"O Lord, my God, how great you are! You are clothed with majesty and glory; you cover yourself with light! ...You use the winds as your messengers and flashes of lightning as Your servants."
(Psalms 104:1-4 GNB)

What is God Saying to You?

◄ *WEEK 5* ►

Are you asking questions of God? Are you getting answers? Are you hearing God? Why can't He be heard?

What God is showing me is that it is important to prioritize my time. I must keep my "alone time" with Him. This divine appointment must be maintained or I could not, would not make it through each day! There is so much busy-ness and loud noise in today's world! All that clamor! Work, family and health issues, marital problems, abuse and financial upheaval, or addictions rob us of His presence. How strong or sincere is our commitment to having intimate time with Father God and His Word? Meditation on (and in) the Word, study and fellowship is a top daily priority for me. First thing in the early morning is best for me! What time is best for you to have daily time with Him?

I work at a ministry called the Ark of Faith Foundation, Inc. We have a service mission that is based on the Scripture: **(Matthew 25:35-36 CEV)** *"When I was hungry, you gave me something to eat; and when I was thirsty, you gave me something to drink. When I was a stranger you welcomed me; when I was naked, you gave me clothes to wear. When I was sick, you took care of me; when I was in jail, you visited me."* In doing these things daily I have learned to stay in God's presence, healing and restoration. It is my belief that each of us encounter God just the same way that Moses, David, Jonah, Peter, Paul, Frances Schaefer, Billy Joe Daugherty, my mother, and countless others over thousands of years did. He's the same God today as He was then!

We have to honor our commitments to spend time with God. I notice that sometimes people get antsy when a worship service takes longer than an hour or if a Christian conference takes an entire day. In some countries where I've visited, I've witnessed people traveling for days to worship and then, staying for days to participate in that worship.

Is my social activity or celebration more meaningful than alone time with God? Is even one day too much time to spend pursuing spiritual healing and renewal to improve our intimate fellowship and relationship? Are noise, glitter and splash the only things that attract us---or are the demands of the world interfering with our search for the face of the Lord our God?

Perhaps I've said it wrong. Every Monday is my fast/prayer day. How I love and enjoy that whole day in His presence! Instead of saying, "I'll fast and pray for you…" Should I be encouraging all of you to fast and pray at least once a week? Should I encourage you to spend that one day in His Word, interceding for others and asking to receive spiritual healing and renewal for your own selves? If we don't ask, knock and seek, the door will not open! Life is delicious and enjoyable. Yes, it's sometimes difficult and I still am not thrilled with "long suffering" but it is a scriptural part of life and we are told to count it all joy… to give thanks in all things! **(Colossians 1:24 GNB)** says it: *"Now I am happy about my sufferings for you, for by means of my physical sufferings. I am helping to complete what still remains of Christ's sufferings on behalf of His body, the church."*

What am I saying and what am I learning? Simply, that I need renewal daily. I need special, all-day refreshment. I need less noise and activity in whirling, fast-flying amusement activities or TV and more time apart, to be with the Christ of God, my Lord and Savior. We all need that. We also need time to receive the Father's love and 'sit on his lap.' Then, I must have the Holy Spirit's comfort, strengthening and help. It's a personal, individual thing but I seem to need, desire and long for His presence more and more! At these times, the struggling, self-seeking pressures of the world fade away and I do find… I know… peace and rest from within.

Finally, trends and contemporary relevancy is actually an indicator of what's going on in our hearts and minds. Relevance is not just chasing the latest new thing. It's about interpreting what that new thing means to each of us, individually. Can we interpret the signs of the times? The Bible shows and tells us most accurately that our three-in-one Holy Trinity produces continual relevance in today's world. In **(Deuteronomy 4:35-36 GNB)**, Moses is told, *"The Lord has shown you this, to prove to you that He alone is God* *and that there is no other. He let you hear His voice from heaven so that He could instruct you; and here on earth He let you see His holy fire, and He spoke to you from it."* The "you" is you and me. He still speaks and we can hear ... if we will only go apart with Him and listen! *"For your heart will always be where your riches are."* (Luke 12:34 GNB)

PRAYER

Father, today I need the help of the Holy Spirit to keep my focus on You. I open my heart and mind to receive Your Words and daily benefits. Show me ways to help others and draw closer to You in Jesus Name. Amen.

MEDITATE ON THESE PASSAGES

Luke 12:15 (GNB) *"And He went on to say to them all, 'Watch out and guard yourselves from every kind of greed; Because your true life is not made up of the things you own, no matter how rich you may be.'*

I Thessalonians 2:13 (GNB) *"And there is another reason why we always give thanks to God. When we brought you God's message, you heard it and accepted it, not as a message from human beings, but as God's message which indeed it is. For God is at work in you who believe."*

Luke 9:49-50 (GNB) *"John spoke up, 'Master, we saw a man driving out demons in your name, and we told him to stop because he doesn't belong to our group.' 'Do not... stop him,' Jesus said. '...because whoever is not against you is for you.'"*

Psalms 68:19 (NKJV) *"Blessed be the Lord, Who daily loads us with benefits..."*

"So then, from now on be obedient to the Lord and stop being stubborn. The Lord your God is supreme over all gods and over all powers. He is great and mighty, and He is to be obeyed. He does not show partiality and He does not accept bribes."
(Deuteronomy 10:16-17 GNB)

Show Me, Lord

◄ WEEK 6 ►

God will show, as well as tell us what He desires of and for us. I have written before that God does "Show and Tell". At that writing moment it was a new concept to me; a new idea. Is God doing "Show and Tell"? Now, as I study Scripture, I circle the word "show" every time I see it! Example: **(Deuteronomy 5:24 GNB)** says, *"The Lord our God showed us His greatness and His glory when we heard Him speak from the fire!"* So, you can see the word 'showed' and in my Bible I circled it. You can also see that God spoke and thus we know He told us something. He is still speaking to us today and showing His greatness! Are we listening? If we have eyes and ears, let us hear and speak God's Word.

Now, back to our example: In **Deuteronomy 5,** the Lord was speaking and Moses was listening! The people were afraid at this time! They said to Moses **(verse 27, GNB)** *"Go back, Moses, and listen to everything that the Lord our God says. Then return and tell us what He said to you. We will listen and obey."* In this present day, we still have pastors, teachers, evangelists, apostles… but Jesus states that we mostly need only a special Helper to teach us: we now have the Holy Spirit! I find that awesome! *"Train up a child in the way he should go … and in his old age he will not depart…"!* **(Proverbs 22:6 NKJV)**

So, how are we training our young people? The ways of this world will not produce joy, peace, love, patience... and the additional characteristics which are the fruits of the Spirit. **(Galatians 5:22)** We need to teach them how to wait for things of value. **(Proverbs 19:12 GNB)** points out that *"…impatience will get us in trouble."* We live in a world of 'instant gratification': frozen dinners and fast foods are affecting our children's health and ours, too. Tweeting and texting while driving are now bringing huge fines, damage and death resulting from accidents in a car and even on a bicycle. In mere seconds we experience 'road rage.'

According to (**Proverbs 19:11 GNB**), *"If you are sensible, you will control your temper..."* You will do it because one of the fruits of the Spirit is self-control. *"Keep God's laws and you will live longer; if you ignore them you will die."* (**Proverbs 19:16 GNB**) *"Do yourself a favor – learn all you can; then remember what you learn and you will prosper."* (**Proverbs 19:8 GNB**) *"Discipline your children while they are young enough to learn. If you don't, you are helping them destroy themselves."* (**Proverbs 19:18 GNB**) Since each child is unique, you do have to provide discipline as God leads and in the ways that work for that child, of course. Still, remember, discipline is part of training a child. Also, use God's "Show and Tell" technique---you have the choice: God's way or world's way.

"Drinking too much makes you loud and foolish. It's stupid to get drunk." (**Proverbs 20:1 GNB**) Training comes by example. *"Children are fortunate if they have a father who is honest and does what is right."* (**Proverbs 20:7 GNB**) It doesn't just mean father, of course. It could be a mother, grandparent, aunt, cousin... well---any guardian. *"Even children show what they are by what they do; you can tell if they are honest and good."* (**Proverbs 20:11 GNB**) Have you ever seen someone "showing off"? Have you seen someone who thinks he or she knows it all? Maybe someone was talking disrespectfully about leaders or "friends"? What is being shown to our children? Remember ... *"a gossip can never keep a secret. stay away from people who talk too much."* (**Proverbs 20:19 GNB**) Train toward the positive and look for the good that is in each person. *"The Lord gives us mind and conscience; we cannot hide from ourselves."* (**Proverbs 20:27 GNB**) Oh yes, *"Sometimes it takes a painful experience to make us change our ways."* (**Proverbs 20:30 GNB**)

Another excellent training comes from (**I Thessalonians 5:12-24 GNB**): *"We beg you, our friends, to pay proper respect to those... who guide and instruct you in Christian life. Treat them with greatest respect and love because of the work they do. Be at peace among yourselves... warn the idle, encourage the timid, help the weak to be patient with everyone. See that no one pays back wrong for wrong, but at all times make it your aim to do good to one another... Be joyful always, pray at all times, and be thankful in all circumstances. This is what God wants from you in your life in union with Christ Jesus. Do not restrain the Holy Spirit; do not despise inspired messages. Put all things to the test: Keep what is good and avoid every kind of evil... Now, may the God who gives us peace make us holy in every way and keep our whole being – spirit, soul and body – free from every fault..."*

PRAYER

How excellent, Lord, if we train ourselves in self-control and bear this fruit before our children. Actions speak louder than words, as we know. We need both Your show and Your tell. Father God, thank you for sending Jesus to set the example so we can be Your example to others in His Name. Amen.

MEDITATE ON THESE PASSAGES

Job 36:15 (GNB) *"But God teaches people through suffering and uses distress to open their eyes."*

Psalms 106:7-8 (GNB) *"Our ancestors in Egypt did not understand God's wonderful acts; they forgot the many times He showed them His love. He saved them, as He had promised, in order to show His great power."*

Deuteronomy 4:11-13 (GNB) *"Tell your children... how the Lord spoke to you from the midst of the fire, how you heard Him... He told you what you must do to keep the covenant He made with you; you must obey the Ten Commandments ..."*

I Timothy 4:13-15 (GNB) *"Until I come, give your time and effort to the public reading of the Scriptures and to preaching and teaching. Do not neglect the spiritual gift that is in you... Practice these things and devote yourself to them in order that your progress may be seen by all."*

∎∎∎ ∎ ∎◄◆►∎ ∎ ∎∎∎

"But the fruit of the Spirit is love, joy, peace, long-suffering, kindness, goodness, faithfulness, gentleness, self-control..."
(Galatians 5:22-23 KJV)

In Fall Harvest Time

◄ *WEEK 7* ►

God is alive and well. He is the Gardener. Daily He is pruning, cutting back the plants. We are the plantings of the Lord! To produce and bear much good fruit, we must be pruned. The dead branches must be cut away and burned up. We must follow Christ's example to lead by displaying what is good and getting rid of the bad. Yes, we must train our children to know the Word. Yes, actions do speak louder than words. We can memorize and speak words but it is in doing His Word that life and godliness are produced. It is by the fruit of character displayed in our daily lives that we give evidence of the reality of the life of Christ within us.

The fruit of the Spirit cannot be hidden. A Spirit-filled man or woman can be spotted by his or her fruit and a carnal man or woman by his or her works. The 'works of the flesh' cannot be hidden. Remember, fruit grows; it is not manufactured. To grow we must *"add perseverance to self-control..."* **(II Peter 1:5-6 NKJV)** Godly character is not built in one day or on one confession of faith. It grows "line upon line." None of us have arrived! Every moment of each day we have opportunity and the choices to grow or stagnate. Look again at **(II Peter 1:5-9 NKJV)** *"...to perseverance godliness, to godliness brotherly kindness, and to brotherly kindness love. For, if these things are yours and abound, you will be neither barren nor unfruitful in the knowledge of our Lord Jesus Christ. For he who lacks these things is shortsighted, even to blindness, and has forgotten that he was cleansed from his old sin."*

Our talents and gifts must be developed. Works of flesh must be 'put off', repented and avoided at all costs. Each of us needs times of refreshing and filling (a *paga*, an encounter with God) wherein we *"repent... and be converted, that our sins may be blotted out so*

19

that times of refreshing may come from the presence of the Lord." **(Acts 3:19 NKJV)**

In recent hot, hot summers I've enjoyed swimming pools more than ever. I love the act of diving in to 'cool off' in the evenings and coming up refreshed. Are you hot, sticky and tired? Each of us needs to dive into the swimming pool---spiritually! We need daily spiritual filling and refreshment no matter who we are. Recall **(Luke 3:16 GNB)** "*... one who will baptize you with Spirit and fire.*" Maybe we need to be re-fired as well. Our refreshing might surely include burning out our sin and turning our hearts to gladness.

PRAYER

Father, prune whatever is dead and unproductive from each of us. Then stir up the flames that come with your lightning-like rods, your arrows (Job 36:32 GNB), and burn away the trash. Holy Spirit, burn up our sinful habits. Let the new life, the blossoms and the fruit come forth in abundance! Now is the time to bear much good fruit. Let it be, in Jesus' Name. Amen.

MEDITATE ON THESE PASSAGES

II Timothy 1:6 (AMP) "*That is why I would remind you to stir up, rekindle the embers of, fan the flames of, and keep burning the gracious gift of God, the inner fire that is in you...*"

Revelations 3:15 (AMP) "*I know your record of works and what you are doing; you are neither cold nor hot. Would that you were cold or hot! So, because you are lukewarm, and neither cold nor hot, I will spew you out of My mouth.*"

Matthew 9:37-38 (NKJV) "*Then Jesus said to His disciples, 'The harvest is indeed plentiful, but the laborers are few. So pray to the Lord of the harvest to force out and thrust laborers into His harvest.*"

Deuteronomy 30:15-16 (GNB) "*Today I am giving you a choice between good and evil, between life and death. If you obey the commands of the Lord your God... if you love Him, obey Him and keep all His laws, then you will prosper and become a nation of many people...*"

■ ■ ■   ■ ■◀◆▶■ ■   ■ ■ ■

"But whoso keepeth His word, in him is the love of God perfected;
hereby know we that we are in Him."
(1 John 2:5 Criswell Study Bible)

Walk In Love

◀ *WEEK 8* ▶

My prayer for each of you reading this is that we walk in love from this moment forward. *"This is how we may discern [daily, by experience] that we are coming to know Him [to perceive, recognize, understand, and become better acquainted with Him]: if we keep (bear in mind, observe, practice) His teachings (precepts, commands). Whoever says 'I know Him [I perceive, recognize, understand, and am acquainted with Him] but fails to keep and obey His commandments (teachings) is a liar, and the Truth [of the Gospel] is not in him."* **(I John 2:3-4 AMP)**

God wants to perfect His love in us! So I am seeking Him in this way: by studying His Word and increasing my desire to have my mind renewed to the mind of Christ. In The Message Bible, the **I John 2:1-5** passage says: *"Here's how we can be sure that we know God in the right way: Keep His commandments. If someone claims, 'I know Him well!' but doesn't keep His commandments, he's obviously a liar. His life doesn't match his words. But the one who keeps God's word is the person in whom we see God's mature love. This is the only way to be sure we're in God. Anyone who claims to be intimate with God ought to live the same kind of life Jesus lived."*

WOW! *"They did not understand that Jesus was talking to them about His Father. So He said to them, 'When you lift up the Son of Man you will know that I am who I am'; then you will know I do nothing on my own authority, but I say only what the Father has instructed me to say."* **(John 8:27-28 GNB)** Jesus saw Him, watched Him, and followed his Father's example!

Please notice that in the Scripture, Jesus did not say it would be easy. I want to paraphrase here how His humanity was shown in the Garden of Gethsemane when He prayed: "Father, I'd rather not be crucified. Daddy, isn't there another way?" In truth, Jesus came to earth with the Father's goal to restore each of us to Himself, God and the Holy Spirit. Jesus' human flesh did not want to experience the pain of spikes in His hands and feet on the cross---or the nakedness!

Have you ever wanted to avoid suffering, pain, responsibility or adherence (obedience) to His Word? Have you ever procrastinated or run away from required, expected duties? Think of Jonah's disobedience and how it caused him to wind up in the belly of the whale! Remember, the children of Israel wandered for 40 years in the desert when the truth was that the Promised Land was only an 11-day hike. Individually, they still wanted worldly comforts and did not want to put away fleshly desires. Had they only been willing to do what God had directed they would have reached their goal in only eleven days!

I followed the guidance of Germaine Copeland in *Prayers That Avail Much, Vol. 1** to personalize the Scriptures as my prayers. Are you ready to pray this prayer of commitment to walk in love?

PRAYER

Father, in Jesus' Name, I thank You that the love of God has been poured forth into my heart by the Holy Spirit who has been given to me. Help me keep and treasure Your Word until the love of You, Father, has been perfected and completed in me. When I am, afraid, remind me that Your perfect love casts out all fear.

Father, I am Your child, and I commit to walk in the God kind of love. I endure long, am patient and kind. I am never envious and never boil over with jealousy. I am not boastful or vainglorious and I do not display myself haughtily. I am not rude and unmannerly and I do not act unbecomingly. I do not insist on my rights or my own way for I am not self-seeking, touchy, fretful, or resentful. I take no account of an evil done to me and pay no attention to a suffered wrong. I do not rejoice at injustice and unrighteousness, but I rejoice when right and truth prevail. I bear up under anything and everything that comes. I am ever ready to believe the best of others. My hopes are fadeless under all circumstances. I endure everything without weakening because my love never fails.

Father, I bless and pray for those who persecute me---who are cruel in their attitude toward me. I bless them and do not curse them. Therefore, my love abounds yet more and more in knowledge and in all judgment. I approve things that are excellent. I am sincere and without offense till the day of Christ. I am filled with the fruits of righteousness.

Everywhere I go I commit to plant seeds of love. I thank You, Father, for preparing hearts ahead of time to receive this love. I know that these seeds will produce Your love in the hearts of those to whom they are given.

Father, I thank You that as I flow in Your love and wisdom, people are being blessed by my life and ministry. Father, You make me to find favor, compassion, and loving kindness with others (name the people you want to include).

I am rooted deep in love and founded securely on love knowing that You are on my side, and nothing is able to separate me from Your love, Father, which is in Christ Jesus my Lord. Thank you, Father, in Jesus' precious Name. Amen.

*Prayers That Avail Much, Volume 1, Word Ministries, Harrison House Publishing, © 1999 by Germaine Copeland, (Scriptures referenced above: **Romans 5:5; Philippians 1:9-11; I John 2:5; John 13:34; I John 4:18; I Corinthians 3:6; I Corinthians 13:4-8; Daniel 1:9; Romans 12:14; Ephesians 3:17; Matthew 5:44; Romans 8:31,39)** *Please read these Scriptures in your own Bible.*

MEDITATE ON THESE PASSAGES

Romans 5:5 (GNB) *"This hope does not disappoint us, for God has poured out his love into our hearts by means of the Holy Spirit, who is God's gift to us."*

Jonah 1:1-17 (GNB) *"One day the Lord spoke to Jonah, son of Amittai. He said, "Go to Nineveh, that great city, and speak out against it; I am aware of how wicked its people are." Jonah, however, set out in the opposite direction, in order to get away from the Lord. He went to Joppa, where he found a ship about to go to Spain. He paid his fare and went aboard with the crew to sail to Spain, where he would be away from the Lord. But the Lord sent a strong wind on the ship... At the Lord's command, a large fish swallowed Jonah..."*

Exodus 15:22-24 (GNB) *"Then Moses led the people of Israel away from the Red Sea and into the desert of Shur. For three days they walked through the desert, but found no water... The people complained to Moses... The Lord gave them laws to live by, and there, he* *also tested them… If you will obey Me completely… I will not punish you."*

Jude 1:1-2 (GNB) *"From Jude, servant of Jesus Christ … to those who have been called by God, who live in the love of God the Father, and the protection of Jesus Christ: May mercy, peace and love be yours in full measure."*

John 14:15-16 (GNB) *"If you love Me, you will obey My commandments. I will ask the Father and He will give you another Helper, who will stay with you forever."*

John 14:21 (GNB) *"Those who accept my commandments and obey them are the ones who love Me. My Father will love those who love me; I too will love them and reveal myself to them."*

NOTES: _____

_____

_____

_____

_____

_____

_____

_____

_____

_____

_____

_____

_____

NOTES: _____

_____

_____

_____

_____

_____

_____

_____

_____

_____

_____

_____

_____

_____

_____

_____

_____

_____

_____

_____

_____

_____

_____

BECOMING PERFECT

DIRECTION: _____

_____

_____

_____

_____

_____

_____

_____

_____

_____

_____

PROGRESS: _____

_____

_____

_____

_____

_____

_____

_____

_____

_____

"Jesus always had the nature of God... Instead of this, of His own free will He gave up all He had and took the nature of a servant..."
(Philippians 2:6-7 GNB)

Called to Follow Christ's Example

◄ *WEEK 9* ►

Each of us is needed to enter a life of servanthood, making the choice by our own free will. We are told to renew our mind to the mind of Christ! Jesus' mind was set on doing the will of His Father God. But don't forget that Jesus was human. Remember my paraphrase of how He even revealed that to us in the garden: "Father, I don't really want to do this. Daddy, isn't there a better way?" That is an example of His humanity. Yet, even after that request, He showed perfect obedience to God by saying, *"Not My will but Yours..."* **(Luke 22:42 GNB)** and still later, on the cross: *"Father, forgive them for they know not what they do..."* **(Luke 23:34 GNB)**

Jesus called us friends! Praise the Lord! That is true. Thank You Lord! One Christmas revealed a deeper understanding of the terms friend and servant to me! At the Ark of Faith Foundation we serve daily and holiday meals. The many people who volunteer to help serve meals and love needy or hurting people in our community on that day exhibited true friendship, both to the needy and to me. I am in my 80s and need friends to serve with me! Did you ever have a friend serve you at a time of need such as a death, illness, wedding, surprise birthday, or even offering a cup of tea or coffee and being present with you at just the right time? As I ponder and appreciate each volunteer's gift of his or her self by going the extra mile or two, I rejoiced! Then I saw more as I read **(Revelation 19:10b GNB)** *"... I am a servant together with you and other believers, all those who hold to the truth that Jesus revealed worship God."* What lesson did I learn? I learned that service is a form of worship.

What does the Bible say is true worship? It says worship is to care for the widow and orphan, feed the hungry, clothe the naked, pray for sick, comfort the dying, and visit those in prison. **(Matthew 25:35-36 GNB)** It means serving someone at that person's point of need. So, I began thanking God that with volunteers, readers and community, all denominations together, we are worshipping our Common Denominator, Jesus. We are serving together with Him---continuing on even in pain or wanting things to be another way. He is the Way; He showed us how!

Later, after the Christmas meal and following my lectionary (reading guide), I read (**Philippians 2:7 GNB**) "*...of His own free Will He gave up all He had and took the nature of a servant.*" We got two gifts: 1) teaching, helping, pastoring, evangelizing for the sake of the body (The Church), and 2) a best friend, Jesus, Who serves each of us daily! It was at that moment when I knew the Scripture on which to base our teaching for the coming year was to be **Revelation 19:10b**: "*... I am a servant together with you and other believers. All those who hold to the truth that Jesus revealed worship God.*"

I re-read (**Philippians 2:1-8 GNB**): "*Your life in Christ makes you strong, and His love comforts you. You have fellowship with the Spirit... kindness and compassion for one another... then... to make Him completely happy by having the same thoughts, sharing the same love and being one in soul and mind... look out for one another, always considering others... taking the attitude of Christ Jesus... who took the nature of a servant... and walked the path of obedience...*"

What a great goal! Together in prayer and supplications, actions and deeds, we make our Lord Jesus happy! We reap what we sow---right? So shall we know happiness!

PRAYER

Father, turn my heart and mind toward Your will and Your ways for Jesus' sake. Amen.

MEDITATE ON THESE PASSAGES

Matthew 23:11 (GNB) "*The greatest one among you must be your servant.*"

John 12:26 (KJV) "*If any man serves me, let him follow me; and where I am, there shall also my servant be: if any man serves me, him will my Father honor.*"

Mark 9:35 (NRSV) "*And He (Jesus) sat down, and called the twelve, said to them, 'If any man desires to be first, the same shall be last of all, servant of all!'*"

Matthew 8:9 (KJV) *"For I am a man under authority, having soldiers under me: and I say to this man, 'Go,' and he goeth; and to another, 'Come,' and he cometh; and to my servant, 'Do this,' and he doeth it."*

■ ■ ■　■　■◀◆▶■　■　■ ■ ■

"Trust in the Lord with all your heart. Never rely on what you think you know. Remember the Lord in everything you do, and He will show you the right way."
(Proverbs 3:5-6 GNB)

What Am I Learning?

◀ *WEEK 10* ▶

Thank you, Father, for Your constant love! I am still learning, even at my age. One example is when I had the opportunity to take the course on Clinical Pastoral Experience Education (CPE) at the Veteran's Administration (VA). I was asked to take it for accreditation. I questioned myself---not God! I knew those classes for rural parish training would benefit all of the Ark of Faith Foundation's work. But could I do it? Could I pass the test? Post-Traumatic Stress Disorder (PTSD) is not only experienced by military veterans, but also by victims of rape, suicide, domestic violence, natural disasters, by children who lose a parent, and more. Even Christians in the army of the Lord get wounded and suffer trauma. What was I learning? Well, it was that I did pass. God knew I would.

Another example came as the winter holidays approached. The Ark was hurting financially. Garry and I paid some Ark utility bills from our own resources. I told no one! However, God never meant for Garry and me to pay Ark bills. He has always provided abundantly for His work at the Ark. We tithe to the Ark and our church. Tithing is relevant and necessary for today, as are miracles. God is the same---yesterday, today, and forever. However, my thinking and pride got in the way, as I later came to realize. People are very generous and thankful during the winter holiday months. The major portion of our year's finances come at this time. I know God never fails us and provides for our needs, if not necessarily all our "wants". What was I learning from this? I was learning that I was inserting lowly me into the business of Almighty God.

As I look back, I was not open with the Ark Board. We had the Treasurer's report monthly except when the Treasurer was away. Could you believe funds were at their lowest when we had no report? I thought, 'Garry and I can do this; we'll catch up later.' Did I count it as tithing? No! It seemed okay to say it was an offering, alms, a ministry safeguard. But, *"Never let yourself think you are wiser than you are; simply obey the Lord and refuse to do wrong."* **(Proverbs 3:7 GNB)** That means we should ask Him before we commit.

Then, a very wise Board Member said, "Sally, I'm putting together a financial committee to study, review and pray with you for Ark finances. We need to free you to do what God has called you to do." Wow! I hugged and thanked him and my Spirit rejoiced. But I still told no one what we had done. You see, God had not led me to pay those bills. I was being led by my own self. I still did not see my pride.

The Ark closes during January so that our all-volunteer staff and Board can rest. When Garry and I have been given January cruises, we rest and God always supplies us in more ways than we can imagine. Jesus went away to rest. He said: *"...leave the ninety and nine... for the one who was lost."* **(Luke 15:4b GNB)** It is refreshing to know that He goes before and prepares the way and also brings up the rear guard! Our prayer for our family and Ark staff when we take these rare breaks is: "Father, rest is a commandment, not a suggestion. Don't let us be so selfish with our rest that You can't use us! Show and tell us what to do and we'll obey quickly. You will get all the glory as we interact with strangers. Since we are available and with You, all things are possible!" Amazing things happen at these times! The last couple of years, He has made divine appointments, *paga*, for us while on a cruise or in a hotel. Once, the appointed individual was deaf and in need of God's love and support. After all these years that He has had me learning and teaching deaf signing, He sent me to the one deaf person on a cruise. I had to leave the 'ninety and nine' because He wanted *"medicine, healing of wounds ...easing of pain"* **(Proverbs 3:8 GNB)** and sharing of the good news and gospel. He wanted me helping one-on-one. Amazing God! Praise You.

Whom God loves, He corrects. Through a series of difficult, unexplainable events revolving around rental property (the source of our personal income) we are learning a deeper level of faith. We are learning to lean not to our understanding, but to His. We are learning, moment by moment, to be forgiving, to drop our attitudes and to practice the gift of self-control. Finally, one night at our regular prison chapel service, I admitted my pride to God and to myself. As I did, God showed me His truth: Sometimes we rob others by not asking for help and allowing them to act. We do it by thinking that we know best.

This moment was the beginning of clarity in my own understanding of the Ark's theme Scripture that year: *"I am a servant together with you and with other believers. All those who hold to the truth that Jesus revealed worship God."* **(Revelations 19:10b GNB)** God was continuing to 'Show and Tell' me to do what He did. He will do the same for you when you ask Him. Jesus sent His disciples out by pairs and in teams. We are not meant to be loners.

An example that struck me as I was writing this chapter is that of veterans with Post Traumatic Stress Disorder (PTSD). Often, veterans and other trauma victims bury their emotions or self-medicate with drugs or alcohol rather than ask for the help of other believers. If they don't lean on God or ask for the help of believers, they find themselves alone with their sufferings in a situation that look like there's no way out. I stopped writing to thank my husband, Garry, a veteran who keeps reminding me that we Christians are in the Army of the Lord. We are veterans too. Christian wounds hurt too and should not be covered up. Ask the Holy Spirit to show you His truth and to make it clear to you! Do read all of **Revelation 19** (in whatever version of the Bible you use) for more about this lesson to worship God together! Please join in our standard Ark prayer now and when you take a break or vacation:

PRAYER

Father, rest is a commandment, not a suggestion. Don't let us be so selfish with our rest that You can't use us! Show and tell us what to do and we'll obey quickly. You will get all the glory as we interact with strangers. Since we are available and with You, all things are possible in Jesus' Name. Amen.

MEDITATE ON THESE PASSAGES

Matthew 14:19-21 (GNB) *"He ordered the people to sit down on the grass; then He took the five loaves, and two fishes... gave thanks to God... broke the loaves and gave them to the disciples, (and the disciples gave them to the people."*

Mark 9:35 (KJV) *"And he sat down and called the twelve and saith unto them, if any man desire to be first, [the same] shall be last of all, and servant of all!"*

Job 5:17-18 (GNB) *"Happy is the person whom God corrects! Do not resent it when He rebukes you. God bandages the wounds He makes... and His hand heals."*

Proverbs 29:1 (GNB) *"If you get more stubborn every time you are corrected, one day you will be crushed and never recover."*

■■■   ■   ■◄◆►■   ■   ■■■

"For when Solomon was old, his wives turned away his heart after other gods, and his heart was not perfect (complete and whole) with the Lord his God, as was the heart of David his father."
(I Kings 11:4 AMP)

Getting on with Perfecting and Maturing

◄ WEEK 11 ►

We are told to come with childlike faith and to keep coming to Father God. Thinking of how we age, the above **I Kings 11:4** Scripture reminded me of the results of loss of faith due to other gods: greed, addictions, doubt, fatigue, and self-destructive thoughts that take our focus off God our Father. It happens to us just like the other cultures' wives and practices took away focus for the kings of Israel. Instead of confessing our sins as David did, with the sincere, contrite and humble heart that God requires, we think we've buried or covered up our sin. Wrong! Father God knows. It took a prophet of God to reveal to King David the demons lurking in his heart. Yes, and what about his consequences? The grace and mercy of God were so great that, once David admitted his choice to commit adultery and murder was sin and fell on his face before Father God, he was instantly forgiven. The Scriptures never tell of any events of David repeating rape or murder. The grace of God was, and still is more than enough to reconcile us!

Thank You, Father, that Jesus gives us power to face any condition (sin) in our past and deal with it! **(Philippians 4:13 GNB)**. We have received the strength not to return to old, selfish ways and behaviors. Thank You, Father, for having Jesus remind us that it is Your will that none be lost, but that all may know You and be saved. Let's review the lesson of Jesus walking on the water. He made the disciples *"get into the boat and go on... to the other side."* He would do the same with us. Jesus set the example by having time alone with God, praying and talking to His Father (our Father). *"Between three and six o'clock in the morning Jesus came to the disciples, walking on the water...'Courage! Don't be afraid!' Peter spoke, '...Lord, if it is really You, order me to come out on the water to You'..."* This was not just any old request. Peter wanted an order, a command! Jesus complied *"Come!"* Then Peter was indeed walking on the water to the Lord---until he took his eyes off Jesus and began noticing the world, the strong wind and the waves. He became afraid and he began to sink. We might call that 'a sinking feeling'! Pay attention to the difference between feelings versus faith. Just like we do, Peter cried, *"Save me, Lord!"* Notice that Jesus reached out at once saying, *"What little faith you have! Why did you doubt?"* (**Matthew 14:22-31 GNB**)

Maturity (perfection) is a lifelong process. We must keep praying to be perfect! We must keep striving for God's perfection rather than being self-determined perfectionists. We must get our minds off of ourselves, our worldly addictions, greed and power! All the money and all the 'things' of the world will not bring you happiness, peace and love. Nor will double-mindedness, doubt and fear. Look what the disciples did in (**Matthew 14:33-36 AMP**): *"... those in the boat knelt and worshipped Him, saying, 'Truly, You are the Son of God! ...and they begged Him to let them merely touch the fringe of His garment; and as many as touched it were perfectly restored."*

This is just like the woman in (**Matthew 9:20 GNB**) who had been bleeding for twelve years and asked only to touch His garment hem to be healed. Perfection (including the process of it) means being "in touch" with Him to be perfectly restored. Worship Father God, Jesus Christ and the Holy Spirit exactly where you are, fully focusing on the Three-In-One who desires to save us right now---at once!

Our part is to work daily, not focusing on what we want for ourselves but as Paul learned and taught. For my life, this means obeying God as explained in (**Romans 8:26 GNB**) *"In the same way the Spirit also comes to help us, weak as we are. For we do not know how we ought to pray; the Spirit himself pleads with God for us in groans that words cannot express."* So I allow the Holy Spirit to use my voice to pray. Paul too, stated, *"I thank God that I speak in [strange] tongues [languages] more than any of you or all of you put together."* (**I Corinthians 14:18 AMP**) In the Message Bible, which doesn't number verses, **Philippians Chapter 4, paragraphs 4 and 5** says, *"Don't fret* *or worry. Instead of worrying, pray. Let petitions and praises shape your worries into prayers, letting God know your concerns. Before you know it, a sense of God's wholeness, everything coming together for good, will come and settle you down. It's wonderful what happens when Christ displaces worry at the center of your life. Summing it up, friends, I'd say you'll do best by filling your minds and meditating on things true, noble, reputable, authentic, compelling, gracious – the best, not the worst; the beautiful, not the ugly; things to praise, not things to curse. Put into practice what you learned from Me, what you heard and saw and realized. Do that, and God, who makes everything work together, will work you into His most excellent harmonies."*

Now that is perfection!

PRAYER

Holy Spirit, I pray that each of us get 'in touch' and submit to God to allow Him to perfect us in His will for the sake of Christ's example. Amen!

MEDITATE ON THESE PASSAGES

I Kings 15:3 (AMP) *"He walked in all the sins of his father before him; and his heart was not blameless (perfect) with the Lord his God, as the heart of David his forefather."*

II Kings 20:2-3 (AMP) *"Then Hezekiah turned his face to the wall and prayed to the Lord, saying, 'I beseech You, O Lord, earnestly remember now how I have walked before You in faithfulness and truth with a whole heart [entirely devoted to You] and have done what is good in Your sight. And Hezekiah wept bitterly."*

I Chronicles 28:9 (AMP) *"And you, Solomon my son, know the God of your father [have a personal knowledge of Him, be acquainted with and understand Him: appreciate, heed and cherish Him] and serve Him with a blameless heart and willing mind. For the Lord searches all hearts and minds and understands all the wanderings of thoughts... seek Him... as your first and vital necessity, and you will find Him."*

■ ■ ■   ■ ■◄◆►■ ■   ■ ■

"But the path of the [uncompromisingly just and righteous] is like the light of dawn,
that shines more and more (brighter and clearer)
until [it reaches its full strength and glory] in the perfect day [to be prepared]."
(Proverbs 4:18 AMP)

A Perfect Day Requires Gospel-style Action

◄ *WEEK 12* ►

Jesus is coming back and we are told, cautioned and warned to be ready. Today's reading schedule from my lectionary was **I Peter 1:13-21** and in my Good News Bible I read, *"So then, have your minds ready for action. Keep alert and set your hope completely on the blessing which will be given you when Jesus is revealed. Be obedient to God, and do not allow your lives to be shaped by those desires you had when you were still ignorant. Instead, be holy in all you do, just as God who called you is holy. The scripture says, 'Be holy because I am holy.' You call Him Father when you pray to God, who judges all people by the same standard, according to what each one has done; so then, spend the rest of your lives here on earth in reverence of Him."* Do read this from your Bible and pray it to the chapter's end.

No one knows when Jesus is coming back; only Father God knows. We are told to prove ourselves. To prove ourselves, action is required. Faith without works is dead, so that means faith with works is alive---it has action. Giving birth is an active process, just like the process of being 'born again'. Perfecting is an ongoing process with God where we work at it daily and strive to ignore our selfish desires and instead do His will for us.

At one time I was a perfectionist, hard on myself and on others. I wanted everything perfect according to my perspective. I now believe I shut out the perfection God wanted. I did not see His will, His Way! Now, as I am aging, still seeking and learning, I am much more committed to daily prayer to become perfect as I allow the Holy Spirit to lead, guide and teach me! Each of us must make our own choices. You and I are not The Perfector. God is. I desire a perfect, blameless heart. Do you?

(Proverbs 2:1-10 GNB) tells us what to do. *"My child, learn what I teach you and never* *forget what I tell you to do. Listen to what is wise and try to understand it. Yes, beg for knowledge; plead for insight. Look for it as hard as you would for silver or some hidden treasure. If you do you will know what it means to fear the Lord and you will succeed in learning about God. It is the Lord who gives wisdom; from Him come knowledge and understanding. He provides help and protection for those who are righteous and honest. He protects those who treat others fairly and guards those who are devoted to Him."* Jesus was sent to show us, to teach us with parables and actions to finish what God calls us to do.

PRAYER

Father, you have stated that You will give us new and creative ideas. Renew our minds daily so that the Holy Spirit can 'Show and Tell' us things to do that day. I request that You send Your Holy Spirit to help readers, friends, students, family, and me to create and develop new ways to serve in our communities. Give each of us ideas now and for future service to be a blessing to other people in their lives. Provide Your innovative concepts that translate into successful and more perfect growth. Encourage us to be blessings to ourselves and others. Use us together Father, according to (Revelations 19:10 AMP) which declares "I am [only] another servant with you and your brethren who have [accepted and hold] the testimony borne by Jesus. Worship God! I pray this be done in Jesus' Name. Amen.

MEDITATE ON THESE PASSAGES

Romans 12:1-2 (GNB) *"So then, my friends, because of God's great mercy to us I appeal to you: Offer yourselves as a living sacrifice to God, dedicated to His service and pleasing to Him. This is true worship... let God transform you inwardly by a complete change of your mind; then you will be able to know what is good and pleasing to Him and is perfect."*

Matthew 5:14-16 (GNB) *"You are like light for the whole world... In the same way your light must praise your Father in heaven."*

Philippians 2:14-15 (GNB) *"Do everything without complaining or arguing, so that you may be innocent and pure as perfect children, who live in a world of corrupt and sinful people. You must shine among them like stars lighting up the sky as you offer them the message of life..."*

I Kings 8:61 (KJV) *"Let your heart therefore be perfect with the Lord our God, to walk in His statutes and to keep His commandments as today."*

NOTES: _____

_____

_____

_____

_____

_____

_____

_____

_____

_____

_____

_____

_____

_____

_____

_____

_____

_____

_____

_____

_____

_____

_____

DIRECTION: _____

_____

_____

_____

_____

_____

_____

_____

_____

_____

PROGRESS: _____

_____

_____

_____

_____

_____

_____

_____

_____

_____

■■■ ■ ◗◀◆▶◖ ■ ■■■

"Do not restrain the Holy Spirit; do not despise inspired messages.
Put all things to the test: Keep what is good and avoid every kind of evil."
(I Thessalonians 5:19-21 GNB)

Do Not Restrain the Holy Spirit

◀ *WEEK 13* ▶

On one of my Monday fasting and prayer days, God sent me to a particular Scripture in a particular translation of the Bible. I obeyed and prayed it over and over with everyone who kept coming and going or calling. I also phoned those He convicted me to call. It was an exciting, rewarding day! It was all to His glory! I only served as a voice. Jesus sent the Holy Spirit to live in us as explained in **(Romans 8:26 GNB)**, where Jesus states, *"...it is better that I go away... I will send the Holy Spirit..."* not just to be with us but to live in us! *"But, it is not just creation alone which groans; we who have the Spirit as the first of God's gifts also groan within ourselves as we wait for God to make us His children and set our whole being free! For it was by hope that we were saved; but if we see what we hope for; then it is not really hope. For who of us hopes for something we see? We wait for it with patience."* **(Romans 8:23-25 GNB)** This means for us to 'keep on keeping on'--- waiting patiently. As I patiently wait for the Holy Spirit's nudging and leading, then *"In the same way the Holy Spirit also comes to help us, weak as we are. For we do not know how we ought to pray; the Spirit Himself pleads with God for us in groans that words cannot express."* **(Romans 8:26 GNB)** He wants to use you, too. So, let go! Let the Holy Spirit use your voice and not just in reading or thinking, but in doing the Word! I know He will *"work all things together for good for those who love Him..."* **(Romans 8:28 GNB)** and He has a higher purpose for each of us! *"So shall My word be that goes out from My mouth; It shall not return to Me empty, but it shall accomplish that which I purpose and shall succeed in."* **(Isaiah 55:11 ESV)** The simple way to say that is: when we speak the Word of God, it will always have the effect He wants it to have. The effect might not be obvious in the time frame we expect, but it will always happen---in His time. Praise the Lord!

We are told to *"leave the company of ignorant people and live"* to *"follow the way of knowl-*

edge." **(Proverbs 9:6 GNB)** Jesus says *"...I'll send the Comforter (Counselor, Helper, Intercessor, Advocate, Strengthener, and Standby) that He may remain with you forever..."* **(John 14:16 AMP)** If He says it, then that is the Truth! Now, go to your Bible and read **Philippians 4:13**. I ask you to do it in your Bible for a reason. Ask the Holy Spirit for help, understanding, wisdom, and strength to do what Jesus says. The surprise to me on that Monday was that I was quoting **Philippians 4:13** as I'd learned and memorized it, as a child. As clear as anything He said, "Read it in your Bible." (I was using the Good News translation daily at that time. I read many other translations, too, for clarity.) Here, I quote myself reading, but when you do it, add your own name: *"I (Sally) have the strength to face all conditions by the Power that Christ gives me."* At an earlier time, I'd printed 'ASK' in the margin, next to **(Philippians 4:6 GNB)**, so I went back to read and meditate on that as well: *"Don't worry about anything, but in all your* (Sally's) *prayers* (fasting day prayers) *ask God for what you* (I) *need, always asking Him with a thankful heart."* In Jesus Christ's Holy, power-filled Name, use His power! Christ gives us commands in present tense, not past tense! Please note that the above phrases in parentheses are my own comments and learnings. If you don't understand, ask for help from the Helper (the Strengthener, the Holy Spirit). Use your voice **(Romans 8:26 GNB)** like I used my voice. This is what happened next:

On my Monday fasting and prayer days, I always hold in my hands the written prayer requests others have given me. I do it as a 'touch point', like they did with biblical handkerchiefs or cloths. For each person and request on each piece of paper, I ask our Father God Who is in Heaven to be present, to let the Holy Spirit lead, guide and 'Show and Tell' me how to pray for this one, in Jesus' Name and according to His Word.

On this particular day, I focused on the power Christ gives to face circumstances with no doubt and no worry. I asked Father God for what each person needed right then. I said, "Father, show me what this person needs at this moment." I began phoning each person over whom I was led to pray. One had a business need, one had a daughter-in-law diagnosed with Stage 4 cancer, one needed finances, and one was awaiting a doctor's call about treatment for recently diagnosed illness… Someone came to my home and, even while sharing and doing this word with the individual present, the phone rang: "Sally, can I come for prayer?" My response was, "Yes, but wait 30 minutes because someone is here and we are praying." So my day went, until I broke my fast at supper time. The Holy Spirit had directed me to pray with people. *"If two on earth agree… it will be done."* **(Matthew 18:19 GNB)** He just kept sending them.

Don't doubt and don't worry what anyone else (including you) might think of your actions. Just speak or do the Word. Face the circumstance by asking your Heavenly Father, God, to handle it in Jesus' power-filled Name and thank Him from your heart. Please read **verses 7-10 of Philippians 4** (remember, I used the GNB and you can use your own Bible). Then practice doing the words. Action is required. Taking action with the Holy Spirit has now become my habit. What about you? Are you ready to do His Word?

PRAYER

Help us, Holy Spirit, to use Your patience as we wait with You for direction and strength for what actions to take from God's Word. Jesus set this example for us to follow. Strengthen us to be faithful to making 'alone time' with You daily and serving others by doing Your Word for them. By doing this in union with You, Lord, I pray that we will continue to grow in joy. The Joy of the Lord, indeed, is our strength! I give thanks, in Jesus' Name. Amen.

MEDITATE ON THESE PASSAGES

Philippians 3:12 (GNB) *"I do not claim that I have already succeeded or have already become perfect. I keep striving to win the prize for which Christ Jesus has already won me to Himself."*

Philippians 3:13 (GNB) *"Of course, my friends, I really do not think that I have already won it; the one thing I do, however, is to forget what is behind me and do my best to reach ahead."*

Philippians 3:15-16 (GNB) *"All of us who are spiritually mature should have this same attitude. But if some of you have a different attitude, God will make this clear to you. However that may be, let us go forward..."*

"Then the people rejoiced, because they offered willingly; because with a perfect heart they offered willingly to the Lord: and David the king also rejoiced with great joy... and blessed the Lord before all the assembly... You are blessed, Lord... forever and ever..."
(I Chronicles 29:9-10 New Heart English Bible)

Perfect Obedience to Father God

◄ WEEK 14 ►

Today all the Scriptures in my daily lectionary readings focused on obeying Father God! First, we had to receive the Holy Spirit, for no man or woman can tame the tongue **(James 3:8 KJV)** ---only the Holy Spirit can. What we say is what we get. Murmuring, gossiping, cursing and the like do not bring joy, peace and love. But when the praises of God go up, His blessings come down!

Referring to Pentecost and subtitled The Day of the Lord, is **(Joel 2:28-32 GNB)**. It reads, *"Afterwards, I will pour out my Spirit on everyone: your sons and daughters will proclaim My messages; your old people will have dreams, and your young people will see visions. At that time, I will pour out My Spirit and even on servants, both men and women."* Then Joel was used by God to warn us of bloodshed, fire and destruction in **verse 32:** *"But, all who ask the Lord for help will be saved..."* Each of us must ask for salvation for our own selves!

Next, my lectionary took me to the Psalms. In **(Psalms 33:18-20 GNB)** we read, *"The Lord watches over those who obey Him... who trust in His constant love. He saves them from death... We put our hope in the Lord; He is our protector and our help."*

That was followed by **(Acts 2:2-13 GNB)**, *"Suddenly... tongues of fire which spread out and touched each person there. They were all filled with the Holy Spirit and began to talk in other languages, as the Spirit enabled them to speak... talking in their own languages... amazed confused... others made fun... saying, 'These people are drunk.'"* (Read it in your own Bible.)

The lectionary readings returned to Jesus speaking in **(John 14:15-26 GNB)**, *"If you love Me,* *you will obey My commandments. I will ask the Father, and He will give you another Helper... He is the Spirit, who reveals the truth about God... Those who accept My commandments and obey them are the ones who love Me. My Father will love those who love Me; I, too, will love them and reveal Myself to them... Those who love Me will obey My teaching; My Father will love them and My Father and I will come to them and live with them ... Those who do not love Me do not obey My teaching. And the teaching you have heard is not Mine, but comes from the Father, who sent Me... the Helper, the Holy Spirit ... will teach you everything and make you remember all that I have told you."* This is His perfection! It comes to each of us as we *"pray without ceasing,"* **(1 Thessalonians 5:17 GNB)** and as we obey and keep our focus on Him. Remember, we only know in part. In my 80s, I am still learning, seeking, asking, and realizing. He wants no excuses but offers daily fellowship and constant love!

Continuing with the **I Thessalonians 5:27** Scripture, I read: *"Peace is what I leave with you ... Do not be worried and upset; do not be afraid..."* Finally, in **verse 31**: *"...the world must know that I love the Father; that is why I do everything as He commands Me."* Does the world know that you love Father God? Does the world know that I love Him?

To practice praying and obedience, I found a lot of help in the book Intercessory Prayer written by Dutch Sheets. Check your library, if you cannot afford to purchase it. I am thanking God daily for this man named Dutch Sheets. Our Monday intercessory prayer group uses this book. Miracles, new awareness and manifold blessings have come. Praise the Lord! The Father gets all the glory!

PRAYER

Holy Spirit, I need your strength and guidance to face all conditions by the power that Christ gives me. Help me through all my troubles. Remind me always that, "Yea, though I walk through the Valley of the Shadow of Death, I will fear no evil for Thou art with me..." (Psalms 23:4 KJV) Thank You for showing each of us that we do get to the "other side"---we get through the trials of this world because You protect us when we are obedient in Jesus' Name, Amen.

MEDITATE ON THESE PASSAGES

I Chronicles 29:17 (GNB) *"I know that You test everyone's heart and are pleased with people of integrity. In honesty and sincerity I have willingly given all to you and have seen* *how Your people... gathered willingly to bring offering to You..."*

1 Chronicles 29:17 (NHEB) *"I know also, my God, You try the heart, and have pleasure in uprightness."*

II Chronicles 16:9 (KJV) *"For the eyes of the Lord run to and fro throughout the whole earth to show Himself strong on behalf of those whose heart is perfect toward Him. Herein thou hast done foolishly; therefore, from henceforth you shalt have wars."*

I Corinthians 2 (THE MESSAGE) *"The Spirit, not content to flit around on the surface, dives into the depths of God ...God offers a full report on the gifts of life and salvation that He is giving us. We don't have to rely on the world's guesses and opinions. We didn't learn this by reading books or going to school; we learned it from God, who taught us person to person through Jesus..."*

I Corinthians 2:6 (AMP) *"Yet when we are among the full-grown (spiritually mature Christians who are ripe in understanding), we do impart a [higher] wisdom (the knowledge of the divine plan previously hidden); but it is indeed not a wisdom of this present age or of this world nor of the leaders and rulers of this age, who are being brought to nothing and are doomed to pass away."*

■■■　■　■◀◆▶■　■　■■■

"But he who keeps (treasures) His Word [who bears in mind His precepts,
who observes His message in its entirety],
truly in him has the love of and for God been perfected (completed, reached maturity).
By this we may perceive (know, recognize, and be sure) that we are in Him."
(I John 2:5 AMP)

Hear, you deaf! ...and See, you blind!

◀ WEEK 15 ▶

"Hear, you deaf! And look, you blind, that you may see! Who is blind but My servant (Israel) or you and me? Or deaf like My messenger whom I send? Who is blind like the one who is at

peace with Me (who has been admitted to covenant relationship with Me)? Yes, who is blind like the Lord's servant?" These **(Isaiah 42:18-19 AMP)** Scriptures are under the header PER-FECT in Young's Concordance.

To be completed or finished, we must willingly, lovingly and obediently finish what He began in us; *"He began a good work in you…"* **(Philippians 1:6 AMP)** Through intimate fellowship we must become responsible for complete obedience---both to God and His appointed authorities. **(I Corinthians 13:10 AMP)** states, *"But when the complete and perfect (total) comes, the incomplete and imperfect will vanish away (become antiquated, void, superseded)."* Our goal is maturity and finished work. The chapter continues in **verse 11**, *"When I was a child, I talked like a child; now that I have become a man, I am done with childish ways and have put them aside."* Naturally, we all understand that this is not just about men. When girls become women, we also have the same responsibility.

In **(I John 2:6-8 AMP)**, we are told to *"walk and conduct"* ourselves, as Jesus did. We are also to realize *"in Him"* the old *"darkness (moral blindness) is clearing away and the true Light (the revelation of God in Christ) is already shining…"* To this I say, Selah! Loosely translated from Hebrew selah means 'to pause and think about that'. The carrying out of God's purposes is the perfecting that is meant by Father God, the Holy Spirit and Jesus Christ the Son of God. Read on through **verse 17**: *"And the world passes away and disappears, and with it the forbidden cravings (the passionate desires, the lust); but he who does the will of God carries out His purposes in his life and abides (remains) forever."* We continue reading this good news in **1 John 2:27-28** *"…His anointing teaches you concerning everything and is true and is not falsehood, so you must abide in (live in, never depart from) Him (being rooted in Him, knit to Him)… Now, little children, abide (live, remain permanently) in Him, so that when He is made visible, we may have and enjoy perfect confidence (boldness, assurance) and not be ashamed and shrink from His coming."*

God wants to perfect us and He also desires intimacy and daily fellowship. This is an inward journey, a personal goal to know God. It must be undertaken for the love of God, and not because a superior dictates that we do it. It must come from the Holy Spirit's prompting, from our readiness to go wherever the Spirit might take us and from seeing for ourselves our true selves in Christ. We do not find Christ at the end of our spiritual journey. He must accompany us along the way. We only need to call to Him. But we must make that choice. We must give and receive and know the reality of being at home in our own selves and not being 'of the world'. We must accept no misleading impressions or simple restless wanderings. Christ's perfecting means He is present in every dimension of our lives. I must know Him, the hope of glory (**Colossians 1:27 KJV**), in my business, church, community, and personal life. I must hear His voice, see Him in earth and sky and sea, and feel His very presence with me. This is what it means to know He is perfecting me---but only if I ask and continue to ask, seek and knock every day. Are you asking, seeking, knocking, and wanting more of your relationship with God?

Christ's perfecting is about a sense of belonging---relationship---and not interior self-exploration. The key is love, abiding love, and the process for each of us to become a more loving person. This perfecting requires active participation on our part. We cannot simply pray a prayer, make a plan, organize or control our thoughts or actions. Instead we must constantly apply the Word to ourselves and the conditions in which we find ourselves. As (**Philippians 4:13 GNB**) states, *"I have the strength to face all conditions by the Power that Christ gives..."* This is true for each of us. It is in the giving and receiving that we are perfected by our Triune God.

Is this prayer below, something you can pray with me?

PRAYER

Father, I long and pray for Your daily encounters---to know you more dearly and cooperate with You, the Perfector who is perfecting me. I want to mature and finish what I started with the Holy Spirit's help and guidance. Reveal all my imperfections and strengthen me to ask for help to rid myself of worldly bad habits, in Jesus' Name. Amen

MEDITATE ON THESE PASSAGES

II Chronicles 24:13 (EEB) *"So the workmen labored and the work was perfected by them... according to design of God..."*

II Chronicles 8:16 (NASB) *"Thus all the work of Solomon was carried out from the day the foundation of the house of the Lord, and until it was finished. So the house of the Lord was completed."*

I John 2:5 (AMP) *"But he who keeps (treasures) His Word [who bears in mind His precepts, who observes His message in its entirety], truly in him has the love of and for God been perfected (completed, reached maturity). By this we may perceive (know, recognize and be sure) that we are in Him."*

■■ ■ ■ ■◄◆►■ ■ ■■■

"It was only right that God, who creates and preserves all things, should make Jesus perfect through suffering, in order to bring many children to share His glory; for Jesus is the One who leads them to salvation."
(Hebrews 2:10 GNB)

God's Goal: Perfect Children

◄ WEEK 16 ►

Watch the tongue! What we say is what we get. Gossip reaps gossip. Angry words bring more angry words. Whenever we say, "I'm not perfect," we are sowing imperfection! Satan uses misleading words and thoughts to cause each of us to abort God's goal. *"What a man thinketh in his heart so is he...."* **(Proverbs 23:7 KJV)** And when those negative words come out of our mouths -- even as Scriptures -- we should remember that, according to **(James 3:10 KJV)**, *"...blessing and cursing should not come out of the same mouth..."*!

Lord, thank you for persevering with me during this study of Your perfecting! I celebrate Jesus with new understanding. None of us truly want to suffer; not even Jesus. Yet, *"although He was God's son, He learned obedience through what He suffered,"* as stated in **(Hebrews 5:8 ESV)** In a different translation, the opening Scripture said, *"It was fitting... that He... in Whom all things have their existence is bringing many sons into glory, should make the Pioneer of their salvation perfect [should bring to maturity the human experience necessary to be perfectly equipped for His office as High Priest] through suffering."* **(Hebrews 2:10 AMP)** Thank you, Father! Thank You, Jesus! The Father 'purifies' people from their sins. Both Jesus and those who are made pure all have the same Father.

That is why Jesus is not ashamed to call us His family. Jesus says to God, *"I will tell my people what You have done; I will praise You in their meeting."* (**Hebrews 2:12 GNB**). Jesus goes on to say, *"I will put my trust in God."* (**Hebrews 2:13 GNB**) He made His choice just like each of us must choose. Jesus continues in that same **verse 13**, *"Here I am with the children God has given Me…"* Jesus became like them and shared their human nature. He did this so that, through His death, He might destroy the devil. He had to become like His people in every way, in order to be their faithful and merciful High Priest. As a High Priest, this was his service to God, so that the people's sins would be forgiven.

PRAYER

Father, thank you for giving me these two gifts: the gift of the Holy Spirit and the gift of faith. I want to please You. Holy Spirit, help me search the Word and illuminate my heart with your truth. Transform me into Christ's image. My desire is to bring glory to You, Father, for Jesus' sake. Amen.

MEDITATE ON THESE PASSAGES

II Timothy 3:17 (KJV) *"…that the man of God may be perfect, thoroughly furnished unto all good work."*

II Timothy 3:16-17 (Williams Bible) *"Scripture is inspired by God and useful for teaching, for reproof, for correction, for training in doing what is right, so that the man (woman) of God may be perfectly fit, thoroughly equipped for every good enterprise."*

II Timothy 4:7 (GNB) *"I have done my best in the race and I have run the full distance, and I have kept the faith."*

I John 4:-12 (GNB) *"No one has ever seen God. But, if we love one another, God lives in union with us; and His love is made perfect in us."*

Ephesians 4:11-13 (Williams Bible) *"He made some apostles; some, prophets; some, evangelists; and some, pastors and teachers; for the perfecting of the saints, for the work of the ministry, for the edifying of the body of Christ… into a perfect man unto the measure of the stature of the fullness of Christ…"*

NOTES: _____

_____
_____
_____
_____
_____
_____
_____
_____
_____
_____
_____
_____
_____
_____
_____
_____
_____
_____
_____
_____
_____
_____

BECOMING PERFECT

DIRECTION: _____

_____
_____
_____
_____
_____
_____
_____
_____
_____
_____
_____

PROGRESS: _____

_____
_____
_____
_____
_____
_____
_____
_____
_____
_____
_____

For both He who sanctifies [making men holy] and those who are sanctified all have one [Father]... I will declare Your [the Father's] name to my brethren; in the midst of the [worshipping] congregation I will sing hymns of praise to You."
(Hebrews 2:11-13 AMP)

God Continues Making Perfect Children

◄ WEEK 17 ►

In the previous lesson, we learned that it takes the entire Holy Trinity to make us perfect. Let's continue with that theme.

Remember that Jesus Christ is the High Priest. *"...He had to become like His people in every way, in order to be their faithful and merciful High Priest in service to God, a High Priest, so that the people's sins would be forgiven. And now He can help those who are tempted, because He himself was tempted and suffered."* **(Hebrews 2:13-18 GNB)**

Lord, I am so grateful that You said, *"However, I am telling you nothing but the truth when I say it is profitable (good, expedient, advantageous) for you that I go away. Because if I do not go away, The Comforter (Counselor, Helper, Advocate, Intercessor, Strengthener, Standby) will not come to you [into close fellowship with you]. But if I go away, I will send Him to you [to be in close fellowship with you].* **(John 16:7 AMP)** Thank You, Jesus Christ. You are *"...the faithful Son in charge of God's house. We are His house if we keep up our courage, our confidence in what we hope for."* **(Hebrews 3:6 GNB)** We must be confident and courageous, confessing our sins and turning away from them; praying to be perfect and not siding with Satan and excusing, rationalizing, or justifying our ungodly behavior.

"So then, as the Holy Spirit says, 'If you hear God's voice today, do not be stubborn... My friends, be careful that none of you have a heart so evil and so unbelieving that you turn away from the Living God. Instead, in order that none of you be deceived by sin and become stubborn, you must help one another every day...." **(Hebrews 3:7-13 GNB)** Oh,

Father, I see more clearly. I see why You sent out disciples in pairs, why You send out ministry teams, why You want us in a church fellowship. We are better together. Thank You, Lord, for giving me responsibilities at the Ark of Faith Foundation. There, I see us daily helping one another! *"For we are all partners with Christ if we hold firmly to the end, the confidence we had at the beginning."* (**Hebrews 3:14 GNB**)

PRAYER

Father, at my age, some days are extremely difficult. I must continue to trust and serve freely, without pay, even as Jesus freely gave. Thank you, Father, for daily "Show and Tell" to do your work with people from pre-teens through their forties. Thank You for giving me the volunteers You have. Thank You for every single one who serves and freely gives to keep the Ark of Faith afloat. Indeed, "in You I live and breathe and have my being." (Acts 17:28 AMP) Help us to receive the Holy Spirit's guidance, perseverance and strength to endure with patient love---at home, church, work, and in our communities. I ask in Jesus' Name, Amen.

MEDITATE ON THESE PASSAGES

James 1:25 GNB *"But if you look closely into the perfect law that sets people free and keep on paying attention to it and do not simply listen and then forget it, but put it into practice – you will be blessed by God in what you do."*

Psalms 111:1-2 (NIV) *"Praise the Lord. I will extol the Lord with all my heart in the council of the upright and in the assembly. Great are the works of the Lord; they are pondered by all who delight in them."*

■ ■ ■   ■   ■◀◆▶■   ■   ■ ■ ■

"But even though he was God's son, He learned through His sufferings to be obedient. When He was made perfect, He became the Source of eternal salvation for all those who would obey Him and God declared him to be High Priest, in the priestly order of Melchizedek."
(Hebrews 5:8 -10 GNB)

So Let the Perfect Come

◀ *WEEK 18* ▶

Jesus, Light of the World, I thank our Father God that He sent You to the earth. Jesus, God's Son, His Very Best, the Perfect One came as Love. His job was to love us back to Father God and the Holy Spirit. His love is constant and unchangeable. The Father's desire is that none should perish, that all should come to know Him and the hope of His glory!

This study is a quest for God's will and knowledge, and the understanding of His consistent urging for each of us to allow ourselves to be perfected by and in His love. At times, I, like a child, had to be made to do or stop doing certain things. I've known His 'tough love' coming full circle to a deeper understanding of the Father's desire for more intimacy in my own journey. Nothing can ever change His love for you, or for me. **(Romans 8:35-36 GNB)** But, clearly, He doesn't always like my behavior. Thus, He continues saying to me, "Sally grow up! Put away childish behavior, talk and thinking."

When my children were babies, I thought each was the most beautiful in the world. I worked with each to develop their talents and gifts. I desired that each be enabled by the Holy Spirit to know God for herself or himself, and become capable adults. Still, a part of me could not fathom how intimate relationships with my adult children could be even greater than the season of childhood I was experiencing at that time. Yes, I am still learning how beautiful and wonderful these adult relationships are, and can be.

Praise God, we are free in the USA to celebrate the Christ of God, the Messiah, Savior, Deliverer, Redeemer, Healer, Sanctifier, Rose of Sharon, Lily of the Valley, Bright and

BECOMING PERFECT

Morning Star, King of Kings, Lord of Lords, Light of the World... Lead on, Holy Spirit! I have great joy in following and loving You! Who will say with me: *"Here am I, send me..."*? **(Isaiah 6-8 NIV)**

To conclude this chapter, I quote **(Hebrews 7:11-28 NIV)** *"...it was on the basis of Levitical priesthood that the Law was given to the people of Israel. Now, if the work of the Levitical priests had been perfect, there would have been no need for a different kind of priest to appear, one who is in the priestly order of Melchizedek, not of Aaron. For when the priesthood is changed, there also has to be a change in law. And our Lord, of whom these things are said, belonged to a different tribe, and no member of His tribe ever served as priest. He was born of the tribe of Judah, and Moses did not mention this tribe when he spoke of priests. The matter becomes even plainer; a different priest has appeared, who is like Melchizedek. Jesus was made a priest, not by human rules and regulations, but through the power of a life which has no end... For the Law of Moses could not make anything perfect. And now, a better hope has been provided through which we come near to God... Jesus became a priest by means of a vow when God said to Him, 'The Lord has made a solemn promise and will not take it back; You will be a priest forever...' Jesus is the guarantee of a better covenant... Jesus lives on forever and His work does not pass on to someone else... He is able, now and always to save those who come to God through Him, because He lives forever to plead with God for them. Jesus, then, is the High Priest that meets our needs. He is holy; He has no fault or sin in Him; He has been set apart from sinners and raised above the heavens... He does not need to offer sacrifices every day... He offered one sacrifice, once and for all, when He offered Himself. The Law of Moses appoints men who are imperfect to be high priests; but God's promise made with the vow, which came later than the Law, appoints the Son, who has been made perfect forever."*

What a marvelous vow and gift! So celebrate Jesus now and every day of your life. Remember, we are told to be like Him. Keep praying to be perfect, strive to be perfect and to accept His correction and chastening. We are being perfected.

PRAYER

Thank you, Father, for Jesus. I do celebrate His life. Thank you for returning us to the Holy Spirit through Christ Jesus. Thank you that in Christ Jesus, I now desire a spiritual walk with You in greater intimacy, a perfected relationship which is always being perfected. Thank you for saving me from being a "perfectionist". Today, I humbly be-

seech all of my readers to continue to ask the Holy Spirit for help to develop and grow stronger in mind, body, soul, and spirit! I ask these things in Jesus' Name, Amen.

MEDITATE ON THESE PASSAGES

Hebrews 9:9b-10 (GNB) *". . . offerings and animal sacrifices presented to God cannot make the worshipper's heart perfect, since they have to do only with food, drink, and various purification ceremonies... and outward rules..."*

Hebrews 9:11-14 (GNB) *"But Christ has already come as High Priest of the good things already here... The tent (our body) in which He serves is greater and more perfect... by the Blood of Christ the eternal Spirit... He offered Himself as a perfect sacrifice to God."*

■ ■ ■   ■   ■◄◆►■   ■   ■ ■ ■

"Make sure that your endurance carries you all the way without failing,
so that You may be perfect and complete, lacking nothing."
(James 1:4 GNB)

All the Way---No Halfway Stances

◄ WEEK 19 ►

As I am being perfected daily, I find things coming out of my mouth but I should not be agreeing with them. Maybe I was speaking with close family or friends and not wanting to 'go there', so I avoided total truth. Why? To keep peace, avoid disagreements and other excuses. However, only truth sets us free. Part of my perfection by the Holy Spirit is to stop, pray, look, listen, and learn. The Holy Spirit corrects and instructs truthfully all the time and all the way. I need to complete the task at hand; face it, rather than going around the same mountain for forty years, like the Israelites in the desert. **(Philemon 4:13 GNB)**

In the same chapter, the Message Bible which doesn't use verses, says, *"Make sure you don't take things for granted and go slack in working for the common good. Share what you have with others. God takes particular pleasure in acts of worship -- a different kind of 'sacrifice' -- that takes place in kitchen and workplace and on the streets."* We must do acts outside the city, camp, church, home, and all the places we go. They must be true acts of sharing, even sacrifice, to cleanse and help people and ourselves rather than seeking to avoid or 'get out of' doing what must be done.

Please go to the book of **James** in the Message Bible and read all of **Chapter 1**! I quote here, *"...Consider it a sheer gift, friends, when tests and challenges come at you from all sides. You know that under pressure, your faith-life is forced into the open and shows its true colors. So don't try to get out of anything prematurely. Let it do its work so you become mature and well-developed, not deficient in any way..."* Do we really know who we truly are until the pressure is on? Until we pass each test, we'll keep going around and around the same mountain, stuck in the same place, doing the same thing over and over yet expecting different results. The good news is that, once we pass each test, we get promoted to higher ground---and the next test. We are being prepared for something great and awesome: *"...God's purpose."* (**Romans 8:28 GNB**)

His perfect way equals learning to love ourselves in a healthy way so we can love our neighbors, family, and friends! We must get rid of selfish, self-centered and destructive ways, habits and speech, abuse, and negativity. We must allow the Holy Spirit to tame or correct our tongues. Why? It's because with the Holy Spirit we can *"...love our enemies"* and even *"pray for them."* (**Matthew 5:44 NASB**) God uses even our enemies to make us into His perfect image.

God wants us to face things, not to ignore or water down or concede to the talk around us. Hateful people and words can be used by God to teach us how to love and forgive *"...because God is always at work in you to make you willing and able to obey His own purpose."* (**Philippians 2:13 NIV**) The Living Bible puts it this way: *"For God is at work within you, helping you want to obey Him, and helping you do what He wants."* He is perfecting us. We need to receive correction and ask for His help to learn the better way, the more perfect way. We are being *"stretched, refined, and pruned to produce more and better fruit continuously."* (**John 15:2 Williams Bible**). There is an *"appointed time for everything... though it tarry, wait for it; because it shall surely come."* (**Habakkuk 2:3 KJV**) Let go, and let God bring things to pass. Do not stop short of your miracle. We have all 'wandered in the desert', felt alone or helpless. That is known by many Christians as a 'wilderness time.' Wilderness times are used to conform us to the image of Christ. It is usually in the most desperate or conflicted times that we encounter God and His loving hand. When we think we cannot live without something or someone, God will show up to show us that in Him we can do all things. He will make a way when there seems to be no way. "*Seek first the Kingdom of God and His righteousness, and all these things will be added to you.*" (**Matthew 6:33 KJV**)

Do you want to pray this prayer also?

PRAYER

Father, as I seek You and study Your Word, illuminate my heart with Your truth. Transform me into Your image so that I might be pleasing to You in all that I do. Have Your will Your way so that I bring You all the glory in Jesus' Name. Amen.

MEDITATE ON THESE PASSAGES

James 1:4 (GNB) "*Make sure that your endurance carries you all the way without failing, so that you may be perfect and complete, lacking nothing. But if any of you lack wisdom, you should pray to God, who wills it to you because God gives generously and graciously to all.*"

James 1:17 (GNB) "*Every good gift and every perfect present comes from Heaven; it comes down from God the Creator of heavenly lights, who does not change or cause darkness by turning.*"

II Peter 3:9 (KJV) "*The Lord is not slack concerning his promise, as some men count slackness; but is longsuffering toward us, not willing that any should perish, but that all should come to repentance.*"

"At one time you were far away from God… But now, by means of the physical death of His Son, God has made you His friends, in order to bring you holy, pure, and faultless into His presence."
(Colossians 1:21-22 GNB)

Enter His Presence

◄ WEEK 20 ►

Without holiness, purity, and faultlessness (perfection), none will see God! Light and darkness cannot be in the same place! If there is light, the darkness is gone. To become intimate with Father God, we must consistently put to death the 'old' man on a moment-by-moment, daily basis. Thank you, Father God, for deciding *"… to bring the whole universe back to Yourself through Jesus' blood."* **(Colossians 1:20 GNB)** *"Christ is the visible likeness of the invisible God. He is the first-born Son… through Him God created everything in heaven and on earth, the seen and unseen things, including spiritual powers, lords, rulers, and authorities. God created the whole universe through Him and for Him! Christ existed before all things…"* **(Colossians 1:15-17 GNB)**.

From the beginning, Jesus is part of the story and plan. Way back in **(Genesis 1:26 AMP)**, God said, *"Let us [Father, Son, and Holy Spirit] make mankind in our image, after Our likeness…"* Look again at **Genesis 1:3-4**, *"And God said, 'Let there be light.' And God saw that the light was good (suitable, pleasant) and He approved it; and God separated the light from the darkness."* Now, go to **II Corinthians 4:6**: *"For God, who said, 'Let light shine out of darkness', has shone in our hearts, so as [to beam forth] the Light for the illumination of the knowledge of the majesty and glory of God [as it is manifest in the Person and is revealed] in the face of Jesus Christ (the Messiah)."*

Read on in **verses 7-17**: *"However, we possess this precious treasure [the divine Light of the Gospel] in frail, human vessels of earth that the grandeur and exceeding greatness of the power may be shown to be from God and not from ourselves. We are hedged in (pressed) on every side [troubled and oppressed in every way]… we suffer embarrassments* *and are perplexed and unable to find a way out, but not driven to despair... (persecuted and hard driven) but not deserted [to stand alone]... never struck out and destroyed... always carrying about in the body the liability and exposure to the same putting to death that the Lord Jesus suffered, so that the [resurrection] life of Jesus also may be shown forth by and in our bodies... that the resurrection life of Jesus may be evidenced through our flesh... death is actively at work in us... [...in order that our] life [may be actively at work] in you... For all [these] things are [taking place] for your sake, so that more grace... extends to more and more people and multiplies through the many, the more thanksgiving may increase... to the glory of God...[a vast and transcendent glory and blessedness to us which will never cease]."*

Satan comes as an angel of light blinding us so we cannot see clearly, but wanting to steal, kill, and devour as we are told in **(John 10:10 GNB)**. It is our individual choice to either crush joy with bitterness and anger by choosing the way of the Prince of Darkness or to focus ourselves on Jesus, the Light of the World!

PRAYER

Father, help us to lean on You and the Holy Spirit. Help us to ask to see through our times of turmoil, stress and resentment so we see it for what it really is. Strengthen us to focus as Jesus did. Help us look up and thank You as He did in Matthew 14:19, when He fed 5000 people. Encourage our belief so we can expect that our miracle will come as it did for Jesus. We need only to concentrate on You and thank You for not leaving us in our mess and humiliation! Thank You, Jesus, for showing and telling us that we know all of our needs will be met. May we see Your glory in the moment. Give us grace to see that same glory even in the face of stress-filled, real-life situations. Help us to know that, in Jesus, we can overcome. You are present in all and through all. You never forsake or leave us all by ourselves. We can face it all (Philippians 4:13 GNB) by Thanking You, once the pain has been exposed. Strengthen us to express gratitude before stress sets in or takes over, in Jesus' Name. Amen.

MEDITATE ON THESE PASSAGES

Psalms 109:30 (GNB) *"I will give loud thanks to the Lord; I will praise him in the assembly of the people, because He defends the poor and saves them from those who condemn them..."*

BECOMING PERFECT

Psalms 30:4-5 (GNB) *"Remember what the Holy One has done, and give Him thanks. His anger lasts only a moment, his goodness for a lifetime. Tears may flow in the night but joy comes in the morning."*

Psalms 30:11-12 (GNB) *"You have changed my sadness into a joyful dance; you have taken away my sorrow and surrounded me with joy … Lord You are my God; I will give You thanks forever."*

James 1:25 (GNB) *"But if you look closely into the perfect law that sets people free, and keep on paying attention to it and do not simply listen and then forget it, but put it into practice – you will be blessed by God in what you do."*

NOTES: _____

_____

_____

_____

_____

_____

_____

_____

_____

_____

_____

_____

_____

_____

NOTES: _____

_____

_____

_____

_____

_____

_____

_____

_____

_____

_____

_____

_____

_____

_____

_____

_____

_____

_____

_____

_____

_____

_____

BECOMING PERFECT

DIRECTION: _____

_____

_____

_____

_____

_____

_____

_____

_____

_____

PROGRESS: _____

_____

_____

_____

_____

_____

_____

_____

_____

_____

■■■ ■ ■◄◆►■ ■ ■■■

"Bear with each other and forgive whatever grievances you may have against one another. Forgive as the Lord forgave you. And over all these virtues put on love, which binds them all together in perfect unity."
(Colossians 3:13-14 NIV)

Perfect Unity

◄ *WEEK 21* ►

God does not show partiality; we are all equal in His eyes. Each of us is gifted and called by the same God to use our gifts for the benefit of the body of Christ. You do not want me to fix your car! Auto mechanics is not in my gift. I love and enjoy being the **(Titus 2:3-5 NIV)** "older woman". Teaching is my gift. I need an auto mechanic to fix my car. You may need a teacher to give you the information to take yourself out of dysfunctional cultural rituals you, or any of us, may have once thought necessary. Some of us even believed that those rituals were necessary for our salvation. Recall Peter, who was shown three times in a God dream in **(Acts 10:9-29 NIV)**: *"...something like a large sheet being let down to earth by its four corners it contained all kinds of four-footed animals, reptiles, birds... then a voice, 'Get up, Peter; kill and eat.' ' Surely not, Lord!' Peter replied, '...I have never eaten anything impure or unclean...' You are well aware that it is against our law for a Jew to associate with a Gentile or visit him. But God has shown me that I should not call any men impure or unclean... so... I came without raising any objection."*

Thanks and praise to You, Father God for always including me and never leaving me alone. It is God's Word that the Holy Spirit will lead us into unity and that we are to help each other become responsible, discerning and well-balanced people in our daily activities. We must ask for help and be doers of His Word. Faith requires action and that practice of Godly principles will enable us to develop healthy lifestyles. *"We warn and teach"* others not to associate with people claiming to be spiritual while continuing to pursue immoral or unhealthy lifestyles. Instead **(Colossians 1:28 GNB)** encourages us *"...to bring each...into God's presence as a mature individual in union with Christ."*

BECOMING PERFECT

If we pray to be perfect, work and practice with and through His Spirit, we will realize His presence both within and among us. We must stay in unity with the Holy Spirit. We need to ask the Holy Spirit's help, guidance and strength to stop using deceitful, selfish and unforgiving behavior. Giving up wrong behaviors and reactions will bring a spiritual awakening to us that is more than just a religious feeling. Instead of shame, guilt, fear, and resentment of the past, we will be connected to the Vine (Jesus) and our future in Him. A spiritual awakening restores our hope and godly dignity. We can develop a healthy self-concept and overcome fear as we participate in vulnerable sharing. Read **Proverbs 18:1** in the **Amplified Bible**: *"He who willfully separates and estranges himself [from God and man] seeks his own desire and pretext to break out against all wise and sound judgment."* Another translation, the **New King James Version** says it this way: *"...the man who isolates himself seeks his own desire: He rages against all wise judgment..."* Still another Bible, the **Contemporary English Version (CEV)** declares: *"It's selfish and stupid to think only of yourself and to sneer at people who have sense."* Now, that's pretty blunt, isn't it?

"No man is an island..." wrote John Donne, English poet. We learn best when doing it together, in association, developing relationships with God and others within the Body of Christ. We must look to The Light and come out of spiritual blindness. We must admit our own immaturity and see our need to ask and receive the emotional and spiritual help of others. We may have been trapped---snared by the words of our own mouths. What we sow, we reap. **(Galatians 6:7 GNB)** Judgment, gossip, blaming, even claiming "no one is perfect" all are equal to sowing negativity and excuses. Instead of sowing unforgiveness, sow forgiveness! Sow truth and reap the truth that sets us free. Sowing the whole truth means giving up selfish delusions such as, 'I don't need any help from anyone,' or 'I can do this myself.' Excuses, alibis and rationalizations for "doing it on my own" or being "self-made" men or women must cease.

Think of Peter in Cornelius' house. From among a large group, Cornelius spoke, *"Now we are all here in the presence of God to listen to everything the Lord has commanded you to tell us... Peter began to speak: 'I now realize how true it is that God does not show favoritism but accepts men from every nation the one who fears Him and does what is right... God anointed Jesus of Nazareth with the Holy Spirit and power... doing good... healing...to preach to the people and testify that He is the One whom God appointed..."* **(Acts 10:33-43 NIV)** We receive forgiveness of all sin through His Name.

My closing thought on perfect unity is that *"...while Peter was still speaking these words, the Holy Spirit came on all who heard the message... and believers... with Peter... expressed astonishment that the gift of the Holy Spirit had been poured out even on Gentiles. For they heard them speaking in tongues and praising God."* (**Acts 10:46 NIV**) Look what God, Jesus and the Holy Spirit can do with perfect unity. That's the power of unity within the Body of Christ!

PRAYER

Father, today I come asking for the gift of faith to be used to encourage unity within the church. May each of us humble ourselves to receive the "more" that You promise is to come. Strengthen us to mature in Christ and practice His example of using our gifts every day. You tell us these gifts are meant to be used together, in assembly, for the building up of the Church (the Body of Christ). Help me rely on the Holy Spirit to remove any barrier to Your wholeness and divine plan. I ask this in Jesus' power-filled Name. Amen.

MEDITATE ON THESE PASSAGES

James 1:25 (NIV) *"But the man who looks intently into the perfect law that gives freedom, and continues to do this, not forgetting what he has heard, but doing it – will be blessed in what he does."*

Psalms 111:1 (GNB) *"Praise the Lord. With all my heart I will thank the Lord in the assembly of His people."*

Psalms 109:30 (GNB) *"I will give loud thanks to the Lord; I will praise Him in the assembly of the people, because He defends the poor and saves them from those who condemn them to death."*

Psalms 111:7-9 (GNB) *"In all He does He is faithful and just; all His commands are dependable. They last for all time; they were given in truth and righteousness. He set His people free and made an eternal covenant with them. Holy and mighty is He!"*

John 17:23 (AMP) *"I in them and You in Me, in order that they may become one and perfectly united, that the world may know and [definitely] recognize that You sent Me and that You have loved them [even] as You have loved Me."*

■■■ ■ ■◀◆▶■ ■ ■■■

"May I perfectly obey your commandments and be spared the shame of defeat."
(Psalms 119:80 GNB)

Spared the Shame of Defeat

◀ *WEEK 22* ▶

"The day of the Lord will come like a thief. On that day the heavens will disappear with a shrill noise, the heavenly bodies will burn up and be destroyed, and the earth with everything in it will vanish." **(II Peter 3:10 GNB)** This will happen! God cannot, does not lie. *"His Word does not go out void."* **(Isaiah 55:11 NKJV)** Continue reading the Good News Bible in **II Peter 3:11-17**: *"Since all these things will be destroyed in this way, what kind of people should you be? Your lives should be holy and dedicated to God, as you wait for the Day of God and do your best to make it come soon – the Day when the heavens will burn up and be destroyed and the heavenly bodies will be melted by the heat... wait for what God has promised; new heavens and a new earth, where righteousness will be at home. And so, my friends, as you wait for that Day, do your best to be pure and faultless in God's sight and to be at peace with him. Look at our Lord's patience as the opportunity He is giving you to be saved, just as our dear friend Paul wrote to you, using the wisdom God gave him. This is what he says in all his letters when he writes on the subject.*

There are some difficult things in his letters which ignorant and unstable people explain falsely, as they do with other passages of the Scriptures. So, they bring on their own destruction. But you, my friends, already know this. Be on your guard, then, so that you will not be led away by errors of lawless people and fall from your safe position. But continue to grow in the grace and knowledge of our Lord and Savior Jesus Christ. To Him be the glory, now and forever! Amen."

Worldly people often teach that, "No one can be perfect---only Jesus." This guide and daily study of the Bible shows and tells us the opposite, based on Scripture. A few of those are:

- **Matthew 5:48 (KJV)** *"...pray to be perfect..."*
- **Philippians 3:12 (NKJV)** *"...not that I have already attained or am already per-*

fected; but I press on..."
- **James 1:4 (NKJV)** *"...let patience have its perfect work, that you may be perfect and complete..."*

We are called to be followers and imitators of Christ and His example. He was perfect. His example was perfection. We are to: *"Be alert. Be on watch! Your enemy, the Devil, roams around like a lion, looking for someone to devour. Be firm in your faith and resist him, because you know that other believers in all the world are going through the same kind of sufferings. But after you have suffered a little while, the God of all grace, who calls you to share His eternal glory in union with Christ, will Himself perfect you and give you firmness, strength and a sure foundation. To Him be the power forever! Amen."* **(I Peter 5:8-10 GNB)**

Thank you, Lord, for perfecting each of us with love! I am just beginning to understand those of my behaviors that, sometimes, God and others do not like---and neither do I. I am so thankful that He never stops loving me and I know that He will complete the good work He began in me. It is an ongoing work! I am asking, knocking and seeking more of Father God. I want His perfection, and I want it in Jesus' Name. I'm still learning **(Psalms 119:96 GNB)** which says, *"I have learned that everything has limits; But Your commandment is perfect."* Daily, I am finding this journey to be more exciting and joyous! I continue to give thanks in and for all things **(Romans 8:28 GNB)** moment by moment.

Please join me in the following prayer.

PRAYER

Father, thank you again for sending Jesus in human form. I am comforted by knowing that He understands human temptation, stress and impatience because of His life experience. Thank You so much for showing me that I do not want to pray for patience---which is only developed through persecutions, trials and tribulations. Thank You, Holy Spirit, that I can ask You to help me. Give me Your patience. Strengthen and comfort me with Your grace. I wait before You, Lord, for Your will, timing and answer. I need the discernment of Christ! Thank You, in Jesus' Name. Amen

MEDITATE ON THESE PASSAGES

I John 2:4-5 (GNB) *"If we say that we know him, but do not obey Him - do not obey His* commands - we are liars and there is no truth in us. But if we obey His Word, we are the ones whose love for God has really been made perfect."

Colossians 1:9-12 (GNB) *"... We ask God to fill you with the knowledge of His will, with all wisdom and understanding that His Spirit gives. Then you will be able to live as the Lord wants and will always do what pleases Him. Your lives will produce all kinds of good deeds, and you will grow in your knowledge of God. May you be made strong with all the strength which comes from His glorious power, so that you may be able to endure everything with patience... and give thanks to the Father, who has made you fit, to have your share of what God has reserved for His people in the kingdom of light."*

■■■　■　■◄◆►■　■　■■■

"Jesus did this to dedicate the church to God by His Word, after making it clear by washing it in water, in order to present the church to Himself in all its beauty – pure, faultless, without spot or wrinkle or any other imperfection."
(Ephesians 5:26-27 GNB)

Jesus, Remove Our Imperfections!

◄ WEEK 23 ►

It is not good for a man to live alone, so *"I will make him a suitable helpmeet..."* (**Genesis 2:18 KJV**) Man needs and must leave his mother and father, says (**Ephesians 5:31 GNB**) *"and the two will become one."* Only in Christ, remaining in Christ, connected to Christ can this be done! We need to keep our focus on Father God, Jesus and the Holy Spirit! It is a journey, a race, and we must cross the finish line. The Word does not go out void, but accomplishes and completes the will and work of God. Holy Spirit, help us make right choices. Both the husband's and the wife's input is required for balance in marriage. Neither is better than the other; they are just different! Read (**Ephesians 5:15-33 GNB**) where we are warned to *"...be careful how you live,"* in **verse 15**. We are told not to do certain things or behave like ignorant people through **verse 19**. In **verse 20**, we are encouraged to *"...always give thanks for everything to God the Father."* This teaching goes on in **verse 33** to exhort husbands to love their wives---and there, the original Greek word used for love is *agape*, which means Godly love. In the same **verse 33**, wives are told to respect their husbands. All of these things are to be done *"in the Name of Lord Jesus Christ."* This came from my daily lectionary reading the very day I was moved by the Holy Spirit to start one of my monthly messages for the Ark of Faith's newsletter.

The message was made more powerful by Scriptures brought to me by a young woman. After lunch at the Ark, this young woman asked to share and pray with me in my office. With Bible still in hand from the noon lunch devotional, I turned to **(Hebrews 12:22-23 GNB)** as she directed me. Read these two verses for yourself: *"Instead, you have come to Mount Zion and to the city of the living God, the heavenly Jerusalem, with its thousands of angels. You have come to the joyful gathering of God's firstborn, whose names are written in heaven. You have come to God, who is the judge of all people, and to the spirits of good people made perfect."*

I started to cry. Father God had just used the young woman to show me several things: 1) She was not aware of my long study of the Biblical use and meaning of the word perfect; 2) as I've been praying with and for her, Almighty God Himself was using "Show and Tell" to demonstrate that she was hearing directly from Him; 3) another newsletter with the perfecting theme was coming; and finally, 4) as I checked **(Hebrews 12:1-3 ESV)**, it became more clear that He is indeed The Perfector! Blood from goats and lambs as sacrifices can't purify you or me. He is working and making us perfect and is doing it as we pray and obey. **(II Corinthians 1:11 AMP)** states, *"While you also cooperate by your prayers for us [helping and laboring together with us], thus [the lips of] many persons [turned toward God will eventually] give thanks on our behalf for the grace (the blessing of deliverance) granted us at the request of the many who have prayed."*

Thanks be to God who, through the leading of Jesus Christ and the Holy Spirit, is completing and will complete the good work He has begun in us. He is the Author and Finisher of our faith. Initially, each of us is given *"a measure of faith."* **(Romans 12:3 KJV)** But He wants us to mature. He is purifying us daily as we choose to spend time with Him. Maturity and perfection come instantly, as we choose to remain in Christ and listen to and obey the Holy Spirit!

I still celebrate the time with that young woman! We prayed together for Him to continue to perfect us and strengthen us to obey quickly! We recognized that we needed each other and learned from and with one another. In isolation, we will not learn; it takes the required *"two or three gathered in His name..."* (**Matthew 20:18 KJV**) Additionally, it all goes along with remembering what (**Proverbs 18:1 AMP**) stated earlier: *"He who will-fully separates and estranges himself [from God and man] seeks his own desire and pretext to break out against all wise and sound judgment."*

PRAYER

Holy Spirit, help us to separate ourselves, not from wise counsel, but from our selfish and childish desires. Open our hearts and minds to see what united prayer can accomplish. Thanks be to God, who is perfecting each of us, as we continue to ask and are willing to be made whole by renewing our minds daily to the mind of Christ and in His Name. Amen.

MEDITATE ON THESE PASSAGES

James 1:25 (GNB) *"But if you look closely into the perfect law that sets people free, and keep on paying attention to it and do not simply listen and then forget it, but put it into practice – you will be blessed by God in what you do."*

John 18:25 (AMP) *"O, just and righteous Father, although the world has not known You and has failed to recognize You and has never acknowledged You, I have known You [continually]; and these men understand and know that You have sent Me."*

Isaiah 61:1-2 (NASB) *"The Spirit of the Lord GOD is upon me, Because the Lord has anointed me to bring good news to the afflicted; He has sent me to bind up the broken-hearted, to proclaim liberty to captives and freedom to prisoners... comfort to all who mourn..."*

1 Kings 8:61 (KJV) *"Let your heart therefore be perfect with the Lord our God, to walk in his statutes, and to keep his commandments, as of this day."*

■■■　■　■◄◆►■　■　■■■

"Do everything without complaining and arguing, so that you may be innocent and pure as God's perfect children, who live in a world of corrupt and sinful people. You must shine among them like stars lighting up the sky, as you offer them the message of life …"
(Philippians 2:14-16 GNB)

Do Everything Without Complaining or Arguing

◄ WEEK 24 ►

I am still receiving the Holy Spirit's leading on the word perfect. This teaching is coming from The Word (Jesus) and the Holy Spirit. Thank You, Father, for Jesus and the Holy Spirit and for Your grace, mercy and love. Thank You, for not giving up on me; for loving me and using me, as You continue to perfect me in Your *"perfect love…"* **(1 John 4:18,** any version) Lead on! I am listening, doing and thus, understanding more and more.

Holy Spirit, I'm asking Your help and strength to develop more skills for discernment. I want to be empowered to motivate others and *"shine like the stars in this corrupt world…"* **(Philippians 2:15 NRSV)** There is much need for people to become truthful instead of complaining and arguing! I do want You to be proud of me so that on the *"Day of Christ"* I will be ready, as **verse 16** continues, *"…and show that all my effort and work have not been wasted."*

My heart's desire is for my readers, family, clients, and the Ark volunteers to make this journey along with me into His perfect will and perfecting plan for our lives. Like Paul said, in **(1 Corinthians 15:31 KJV)**, we must learn to *"die daily…"* Our human nature would often crave its own way. It complains and argues when its own personal desires are not met. Thank you, Father, for loving us at all times---even when You are correcting us and requiring repentance to make us perfect. Your work in us and with us mandates obedient change. You may not always like us or our behavior, but Your love, agape for us is constant.

(Proverbs 4:10-27 GNB) says, *"Listen to Me, my child. Take seriously what I am telling you… I have taught you wisdom and the right way to live. Nothing will stand in your way* *if you walk wisely... always remember what you have learned. Your education is your life---guard it well. Do not go where evil people go. Do not follow the example of the wicked. Don't do it! Keep away from evil! Refuse it and go on your way... The road the righteous travel is like the sunrise, getting brighter and brighter... My child, pay attention to what I say. Listen to My words. Never let them get away from you. Remember them and keep them in your heart. They will give life and health... Be careful how you think; your life is shaped by your thoughts. Never say anything that isn't true. Have nothing to do with lies and misleading words... Plan carefully what you do and whatever you do will turn out right. Avoid evil and walk straight ahead. Don't go one step off the right way."*

We must avoid complaining and the arguments which follow. Avoid lies that burst forth as we say "never" and "always" or words that blame others. Words accompanying "never" and "always" usually are misleading, as are accusing phrases like, "You never..." and "I always..." Rarely are we that extreme. Truth is God's way! Truth keeps us pure. God desires truth in His perfect children.

PRAYER

Father, examine the sincerity of my heart. Holy Spirit, help me adjust and correct my human spirit. Today, in Jesus' Name, I ask You, Holy Spirit, to completely and fully direct my life by the grace of God, Amen.

MEDITATE ON THESE PASSAGES

I John 4:17 (ESV) *"Love is made perfect in us in order that we may have courage on Judgment Day; and we will have it because our life in this world is the same as Christ's."*

I John 4:18 (ESV) *"There is no fear in Love; perfect Love drives out all fear. So then, love has not been made perfect in anyone who is afraid, because fear has to do with punishment."*

Matthew 5:48 (NIV) *"Be perfect, therefore, as your Heavenly Father is perfect."*

1 Chronicles 22:19 (AMPC) *"Set your mind and heart to seek (inquire of and require as your vital necessity) the Lord your God..."*

NOTES: _____

DIRECTION: _____

_____

_____

_____

_____

_____

_____

_____

_____

_____

PROGRESS: _____

_____

_____

_____

_____

_____

_____

_____

_____

_____

■■■ ■ ◨◀◆▶◨ ■ ■■■

"Oh Lord, You are my God, I will exalt you and Praise Your name, for in perfect faithfulness You have done marvelous things, things planned long ago."
(Isaiah 25:1 NIV)

Glory To The Righteous One

◄ *WEEK 25* ►

Precious heavenly Father, One and only true God, thank You for Jesus, Your wonderful Son. Thank You for restoring the Holy Spirit to live in each of us. Thank You for daily perfecting us in Your Fatherly love! **(Romans 8:28 AMP)** applies: *"We are assured and know that [God being a partner in their labor] all things work together and are [fitting into a plan] for good to those who love God and are called according to [His] design and purpose."*

Another day, God sent another young woman to encourage me in this study of the meaning of perfect. **The Good News Bible** was the version for my daily study. I have numerous translations and use them for study and Ark of Faith newsletters. The *"perfect faithfulness"* of God was presented on that Friday night at the Ark's Lamplighter Coffeehouse by students from our local Bacone College. Father, I do so love and bless You and enjoy these young people You place in my life. You know that well! Thank You!

The Father had planned this paga, this meeting, at the coffeehouse. As I shared what He was teaching me, He revealed more through a new friend in Christ who used her **New International Version (NIV) Bible.** He planned this long ago! Together we are better. We grow and become more mature. As I turned to **Isaiah 25:1** in my **GNB,** I read the words, *"You faithfully carried out the plans You made long ago …"* You made us -- the Ark of Faith -- into Your safe place and storehouse as *"...the poor and helpless have fled to You and have been safe in time of trouble. You give them shelter from storms. And shade from burning heat..."* **(Isaiah 25:4, also GNB)** In the "dog days" of Oklahoma summers, the Ark is also a respite from the burning heat as God's poor and helpless come to us for shelter.

Father, thank You also for having sent my new friend in Christ with her handwritten note stating the above Scripture as God's purpose and promise of more. What does God have in store for each of us who provide *"...refuge for the poor, a refuge for the needy in distress..."*? **(Isaiah 25:4 NIV)**

Alone, I cannot do all that must be done at, through and for the Ark of Faith Foundation. As I age, I am greatly encouraged by the people You send to complete the *"good work You began in me"* long ago. *"I do not claim that I have already succeeded or have already become perfect. I keep striving to win the prize for which Christ Jesus has already won me to Himself... the one thing I do, however, is to forget what is behind me and do my best to reach what is ahead..."* **(Philippians 2:12-14 GNB)** God does not get side tracked and every day is helping to keep me focused through the Holy Spirit and the people He sends. These seemingly unplanned meetings greatly encourage me and so I encourage them.

Finally for today, *"You will keep in perfect peace him whose mind is steadfast, because He trusts in you. Trust in the Lord forever, for the Lord, the Lord is the Rock eternal."* **(Isaiah 26:3-4 NIV)**

PRAYER

What is next? Lead on, Holy Spirit. Your will and mine are becoming one. It's exciting, as You send 'perfect' strangers to add to my knowledge. How wonderful and magnificent are Your ways. With You, there are no half-way journeys. Each of us must cooperate with You. Father, Help us to finish the good work You began in us, in Jesus' Name. Amen.

MEDITATE ON THESE PASSAGES

I John 4:12 (GNB) *"No one has ever seen God, but if we love one another, God lives in union with us, and His love is made perfect in us."*

I John 4:17 (ESV) *"Love is made perfect in us in order that we may have courage on Judgment Day; and we will have it because our life in this world is the same as Christ's."*

1 John 4:18 (ESV) *"There is no fear in love; perfect love drives out all fear. So then, love has not been made perfect in anyone who is afraid, because fear has to do with punishment."*

Isaiah 24:16 (NIV) *"Remember to always sing: Glory to the Righteous One."*

I Kings 8:61 (KJV) *"Let your heart therefore be perfect with the Lord our God, to walk in his statutes, and to keep his commandments, as at this day."*

■■■　■　■◀◆▶■　■　■■■

"Keep me safe also from willful sins; don't let them rule over me. Then I shall be perfect and free from the evil of sin."
(Psalms 19:13 GNB)

The Law of The Lord Is Perfect

◀ WEEK 26 ▶

Father, help us to be at rest from all self-seeking and to be obedient to your law. In **(Proverbs 28:9 GNB)** we are reminded that *"...if we do not obey the law, God will find our prayers too hateful to hear."* Today, some of our man-made laws are against God's law and our own opinions and senses often deceive us. A good conscience and virtuous life are preferred! Our endeavor should be to practice self-control---which is a fruit (benefit) of the Spirit. Help us, Holy Spirit, to make progress toward forsaking our own wills and learn to do Your will.

True peace is found by resisting our passions and obeying our Father God. Outward comforts, conflicting thoughts and conversations with others may cause a great loss to our peace of mind. Holy Spirit, help us to *"...watch and pray."* **(Matthew 26:41 GNB)** Strengthen us to control ourselves toward the Father's will instead of toward transitory things and passions. I want to obtain divine comfort and peace and be willing to let go of my plan and let God help me more every day. I am so glad He is the Perfector and not my self-willed controlling ways of 'perfectionism.' I want to enter into His perfect will and path! I need the strength of Christ to face conditions and circumstances in my own life and root out the vices and evils in it **(Philippians 4:13 GNB)** in order to become that perfect person He wants. I am still praying to be perfect as He wants and am intentionally surrendering to His will.

BECOMING PERFECT

After all these years, I know that perfect security and peace cannot exist in the world. Temptations are troublesome, but can turn profitable when we allow ourselves to become humbled, purified and instructed by the Helper. Running away from temptations does not help us overcome them. Facing temptations with the Holy Spirit's strength and help secures victory over them. God's help, patience, long-suffering, and even His comforting are what eventually bring us victory.

We cannot be careless. We must spend time alone with Father God! Holy Spirit, strengthen each of us to quickly resist temptation in our areas of weakness. The slower we are to resist, the weaker we become. **(I Peter 5:6-11 NIV)** So, *"humble yourself, therefore, under God's mighty hand, that He may lift you up in due time... be self-controlled and alert. Your enemy, the devil, prowls around like a roaring lion looking for someone to devour. Resist him, standing firm in the faith, because you know your brothers throughout the world are undergoing the same kind of sufferings. And the God of all grace, to His eternal glory in Christ, after you have suffered a little while, will Himself restore you and make you strong, firm and steadfast. To Him be the power forever and ever. Amen."* When you choose Him over temptation, He will give you the strength you need to avoid giving in to it. Obedience to God is not our natural reaction, so we truly must stop, think and make that decision every time---until it becomes our response by habit.

PRAYER

Holy Spirit, kindle within me, each member of my family and Christian community the desire to love more. To paraphrase (Mark 12:30-31 AMP): help me to love the Lord God with all my heart, with all my soul, with all my mind, and with all my strength and to love my neighbor as I love myself, in Jesus' Name. Amen.

MEDITATE ON THESE PASSAGES

Psalms 19:7 (CEV) *"The Law of the Lord is perfect; it gives us new life. His teachings last forever; and they give wisdom to ordinary people."*

Psalms 18:25 (GNB) *"O Lord, You are faithful to those who are faithful to You; completely good to those who are perfect."*

I Corinthians 13:4-5 (GNB) *"Love is patient and kind; it is not jealous or conceited, or proud; love is not ill-mannered or selfish or irritable; love does not keep record of wrongs ..."*

Revelation 2:7 (NIV) *"He who has an ear, let him hear what the Spirit says to the churches. To him who overcomes I will give the right to eat from the tree of life, which is in the paradise of God."*

Hebrews 9:14 (GNB) *"Since this is true, how much more is accomplished by the blood of Christ! Through the eternal Spirit, Jesus offered Himself as a perfect sacrifice to God. His blood will purify our consciences from useless rituals so we may serve the living God."*

■ ■ ■　　■　 ◄ ◆ ►　 ■　　 ■ ■ ■

"Don't be deceived, my dear brothers. Every good and perfect gift is from above, coming down from the Father of Heavenly lights, Who does not change like shifting shadows."
(James 1:16-17 NIV)

Father Perfectly Instructs Me

◄ WEEK 27 ►

Lord Jesus, You alone are my heart's desire! Today, I chose to fast and pray so I could be about my Father's business as His servant. So much is going on around me---decisions to be made, people hurting, young people still needing the **(Titus 2:3-5 GNB)** "older woman." My husband Garry and I were participating in more training for our work with U.S. military veterans. We know that this PTSD class is for the Lord's army, too. We must hear from You, Father, and focus on Your will and Your way.

My Monday fasting day has become my Sabbath; a great joy and strength in my life. Suddenly, it was not Monday, but I knew I needed to fast and pray today, an extra day. As I uttered, "Yes, Lord," I reached for my Bible and found I'd left it in the car the night before. Then I saw my old copy of Thomas à Kempis' book *The Imitation of Christ* and I picked it up.

BECOMING PERFECT

I had been revisiting earlier books and readings and finding greater awareness. This day, I found that book from a past spiritual journey. Thomas à Kempis speaks this word 'perfect' often. During my study of 'perfect', I see God's hand and His leading in my life from many years ago.

I turned to where I had last left off reading and the very first line was, *"I will hear what God the Lord will speak..."* **(Psalms 85:8 KJV)** There à Kempis remarks that people are blessed when they gladly make time for God and shake off all worldly hindrances. I want to hear God and the Holy Spirit more, to make better use of my spare time and to willing shake off hindrances. Thank you Father, for this man who shared his daily steps following Christ! Holy Spirit, I want to follow Christ as Thomas did!

Like à Kempis, I want to attain true blessedness. Do you? We are not alone. Quoting from **(I Samuel 3:9 NIV)**, Thomas compared himself to Samuel who says, *"Speak Lord... for your servant is listening..."* Following Thomas' leading, I read **(Psalms 119:124-125 NIV)**, *"Deal with your servant according to your love and teach me your decrees. I am your servant; give me discernment that I may understand your statutes..."* à Kempis used these Scriptures to point out that it is not Moses, the prophets, or any man, but the Lord God -- the Inspirer and Enlightener of all prophets -- that could perfectly instruct him. Why? So that clarification can come to each of us, as God gives *"...understanding, that I may know Thy testimonies."* **(Psalms 119:125 KJV)** God loved us so much that He gave Jesus to help us understand. We have the mind of Christ just like Thomas à Kempis did.

Today, mighty men and women of God are used to point me to the Word, to His truth. Yet, only Father God, through the Holy Spirit in Jesus' Name, can perfectly instruct us. Thomas à Kempis wrote, *"Some declare commandments but Thou help us fulfill them."* Godly men and women point the way but Christ alone strengthens us to do all things. **(Philippians 4:13 GNB)** Christ gives us the power to face daily pains, evils, struggles, and temptations. Simon Peter also affirmed this in **(John 6:68-69 GNB)** when he said, *"Lord, to whom would we go? You have the words that give eternal life. And now we believe and know that You are the Holy One who has come from God."*

If you can agree with this concept, you may want to fast, but if you do or don't, please pray with me.

PRAYER

No man, no woman---only You, Lord Jesus, give perfect instruction for the living of our lives in today's world. Thank You for nudging me, whispering for me to come closer and spend more time with You today, fasting and praying for Your sake. Amen.

MEDITATE ON THESE PASSAGES

Mark 13:11 (GNB) *"And when you are arrested and taken to court, do not worry ahead of time, about what you are going to say; when the time comes, say whatever is then given you. For the words you speak will not be yours; they will come from the Holy Spirit."*

Hebrews 9:11 (NIV) *"Christ came as high priest of the good things that are already here, He went through the greater and more perfect tabernacle that is not man-made, that is to say, not a part of this creation."*

Matthew 5:48 (NIV) *"Be perfect, therefore, as your heavenly Father is perfect."*

Psalms 119:96 (GNB) *"I have learned that everything has limits; but Your commandment is perfect."*

■ ■ ■   ■   ■◄◆►■   ■   ■ ■ ■

"For He says, 'In the time of my favor I heard you, and in the day of salvation I helped you.' I tell you, now is the time of God's favor, now is the day of salvation."
(II Corinthians 6:2 NIV)

May God Be With You In Everything You Do

◄ WEEK 28 ►

Today I ask the Holy Spirit to strengthen and help us spend more time with the Father and celebrate the gift of Jesus Christ. I ask for His help for us to avoid the snare of too many worldly activities and miss His will for today. We must amend our ways and free ourselves so we can enjoy and profit from our fellowship. We need the Holy Spirit's strength to order every act and thought so that we can live and die with Christ. **Romans 6:8-9** reveals that when Paul recognized what Jesus had done for him by dying, his heart changed from that of one living in sin and became a perfectly contrite heart that was dead to sin. We need the Holy Spirit's help to rise above pride, presumptions and any illusions that good work alone brings true salvation. We need that help to move in purity and service as we begin to walk more perfectly. We need that strength to live as Christ did and willingly forgive the offenses of others. Like Christ, I want to do more acts of kindness while sharing this good news.

"For I am convinced that neither death nor life, neither angels nor demons, neither the present nor the future, nor any powers, neither height nor depth, nor anything else in all creation will be able to separate us from the love of God that is in Christ Jesus our Lord." **(Romans 8:38-39 NIV)** What we need is the perfect love of God that **I Corinthians 13** describes. I added it at the end of this chapter. It is what He intends for those of us who receive His son. We are supposed to delight in Jesus! We are called to be fervent in worship and serving others as in **Matthew 25:35-36**... feeding, clothing, comforting, praying, and visiting. Then *"...the King will reply, I tell you the truth, whatever you did for one of the least of these brothers of mine, you did it for Me."* **(Matthew 25:40 NIV)** This is the true way to celebrate Christ!

"Behold, now is truly the time for a gracious welcome and acceptance [of you from God]; behold, now is the day of salvation..." **(II Corinthians 6:2b AMP)** We must ask for the Holy Spirit's help to free ourselves from worldly lusts and vanity---illusions of riches and grandeur---and start living in daily intimacy with Christ. All who see Jesus see the Father. This same Jesus restored the Holy Spirit of God to each of us who are willing to receive by faith. We must labor and pray to be perfect---to submit our flesh to the Spirit. *"Therefore, I urge you, brothers, in view of God's mercy, to offer your bodies as living sacrifices, holy and pleasing to God – this is your spiritual act of worship. Do not conform any longer to the patterns of this world, but be transformed by the renewing of your mind. Then you will be able to test and approve what God's will is – His good, pleasing and perfect will."* **(Romans 12:1-2 NIV)**.

Remember, *"No one has seen God, but if we love one another, God lives in union with us, and His love is made perfect in us."* **(I John 4:12 GNB)** May we, like Paul, be able to say,

"My conscience is perfectly clear about the way which I have lived before God to this very day." **(Acts 23:1 GNB)**

PRAYER

Holy Spirit, help us reflect God's love today. Strengthen us to pray for and love our enemies. Help each of us to simplify and simply share the love of Christ with family and friends in our homes and lives! Help us to do it in Jesus' Name. Amen.

MEDITATE ON THESE PASSAGES

I Chronicles 28:9 (KJV) *"...know thou the God of thy father and serve Him, with a perfect heart... a willing mind; for the Lord searches all hearts and understandeth all the imaginations of the thoughts, if thou seeketh Him...*

Revelations 3:2 (NIV) *"So wake up, and strengthen what you still have before it dies completely. For I find that what you have done is not yet perfect in the sight of God."*

Isaiah 25:1 (NIV) *"O Lord, you are my God; I will exalt you and praise your name, for in perfect faithfulness you have done marvelous things, things planned long ago."*

Isaiah 26:3-4 (NIV) *"You will keep in perfect peace him whose mind is steadfast, because he trusts in You. Trust in the Lord forever, for the Lord, The Lord, is the Rock eternal."*

I Corinthians 13 (NKJV) *"Though I speak with the tongues of men and of angels, but have not love, I have become sounding brass or a clanging cymbal. 2 And though I have the gift of prophecy, and understand all mysteries and all knowledge, and though I have all faith, so that I could remove mountains, but have not love, I am nothing. 3 And though I bestow all my goods to feed the poor, and though I give my body to be burned, but have not love, it profits me nothing. 4 Love suffers long and is kind; love does not envy; love does not parade itself, is not puffed up; 5 does not behave rudely, does not seek its own, is not provoked, thinks no evil; 6 does not rejoice in iniquity, but rejoices in the truth; 7 bears all things, believes all things, hopes all things, endures all things. 8 Love never fails. But whether there are prophecies, they will fail; whether there are tongues, they will cease; whether there is knowledge, it will vanish away. 9 For we know in part and we prophesy in part. 10 But when that which is perfect has come, then that which is in part will be done away. 11 When I was a child, I spoke as a child, I understood as a child, I thought as a* *child; but when I became a man, I put away childish things. 12 For now we see in a mirror, dimly, but then face to face. Now I know in part, but then I shall know just as I also am known. 13 And now abide faith, hope, love, these three; but the greatest of these is love."*

NOTES: _____

_____

_____

_____

_____

_____

_____

_____

_____

_____

_____

_____

_____

_____

_____

_____

_____

_____

DIRECTION: _____

_____
_____
_____
_____
_____
_____
_____
_____
_____
_____
_____

PROGRESS: _____

_____
_____
_____
_____
_____
_____
_____
_____
_____
_____

"The Almighty God, the Lord, speaks; He calls to the whole earth from east to west. God shines from Zion, the city, perfect in its beauty."
(Psalms 50:1-2 GNB)

The Perfection of Beauty

◄ WEEK 29 ►

What now, Lord? Is there more? In my research, I turned to **Psalms 50:1-2** in the **Amplified Bible** and read that beginning Scripture in a different translation, *"The Mighty One, God, the Lord, speaks and calls the earth from the rising of the sun to its setting. Out of Zion, the perfection of beauty, God shines forth."* Is Zion really the 'perfect' city? Well, I do know that God loves and creates beauty...

In the beginning God made a perfectly beautiful garden---Eden. All that He made was good! He brought order out of chaos. Adam was told not to eat of the one tree. But both Adam and Eve ate of it – and sin entered into the garden because they disobeyed. The perfection God had made became chaotic and ugly. The same way, as sin increases in our cities and families, beauty is lost in darkness. **(Romans 12:2 GNB)** tells us, *"Do not conform yourselves to the standards of this world, but let God transform you inwardly by a complete change of your mind. Then you will be able to know the Will of God... what is good and is pleasing to Him and is perfect."*

The will of God is to transform us from the inside out. Then Christ in us -- the Holy Spirit living in us -- will resist this world's lack of Godly standards. The beauty, the perfection God desires for each of us is made completely perfect in Christ. Look at **(Romans 12:1 GNB)**: *"So then my friends, because of God's great mercy to us, I appeal to you: Offer yourselves as a living sacrifice to God, dedicated to His service and pleasing to Him. This is the true worship that you should offer."* How beautiful our cities and our families would be if we all served Him at all times.

Keep reading in **Romans 12**: *"Do not think of your selves more highly than you should. In-*

stead, judge yourself according to the amount of faith God has given you... So we are to use our different gifts in accordance with the grace that God has given us." In union with Christ, joined together, all our different gifts become one glorious, beautiful whole. In Christ (the "sincere love of Christ") we are told to *"Hate what is evil; hold on to what is good. Love one another warmly as Christians, and be eager to show respect for one another. Work hard and do not be lazy."* **(Romans 12:3-11 GNB)**

Strong's Bible Dictionary defines grace as 'beauty' and 'well-favored' both in Hebrew and Chaldean. The Armenian term is the most used form of the word grace, especially in Jesus' new covenant. It means the 'favor of the Lord Jesus Christ' -- a spiritual act -- *"the divine influence upon the heart and its perfection in the life."* That means spiritually taking Jesus into our hearts and reflecting Him in our daily lives. The Greek meaning is also used in the new covenant and includes graciousness as 'gratifying', a manner of action or spiritual movement. So you can see that the divine influence of the heart means that your life becomes a reflection of His, which *"...includes gratitude, acceptable benefit, favor, gifts, joy, liberality, pleasure and thank-worthiness."*

Noah and people of his era found grace in the old covenant. Then, Christ brought the new covenant's transformation by the spiritual influence of grace, a free gift to us. Grace is so much more than 'unmerited favor.' Without Christ's and the Holy Spirit's influence on and in our hearts and creating a lifestyle change, there would be no true joy! With only worldly desires, we would remain in darkness and chaos. However, **Chapters 1-4 of Philippians** say that joy now rules! Read it in your own Bible and thank God for giving us Jesus.

PRAYER

I pray for Christ and His Holy Spirit to influence the readers' hearts, families, cities, states and nations to this new covenant definition of grace! Holy Spirit, help me recognize and receive this grace so that I will bring Your fruits of peace, joy, love, gentleness, kindness, and patience everywhere I go. Then, in Christ, the 'beautiful city' will again be visible and gang wars and violence will disappear. This I pray in Jesus' Name, Amen.

MEDITATE ON THESE PASSAGES

Philippians 1:2 (GNB) *"May God our Father and the Lord Jesus Christ give you grace and peace."*

BECOMING PERFECT

Philippians 1:9-10 (GNB) *"I pray that your love will keep on growing more and more, together with true knowledge and perfect judgment, so that you will be able to choose what is best. Then you will be free from all impurity and blame on the Day of Christ."*

Philippians, Chapter 1 (THE MESSAGE *[but read it in your own])* *"1 And that's about it, friends. Be glad in God! I don't mind repeating what I have written in earlier letters, and I hope you don't mind hearing it again. Better safe than sorry—so here goes. 2-6 Steer clear of the barking dogs, those religious busybodies, all bark and no bite. All they're interested in is appearances—knife-happy circumcisers, I call them. The real believers are the ones the Spirit of God leads to work away at this ministry, filling the air with Christ's praise as we do it. We couldn't carry this off by our own efforts, and we know it—even though we can list what many might think are impressive credentials. You know my pedigree: a legitimate birth, circumcised on the eighth day; an Israelite from the elite tribe of Benjamin; a strict and devout adherent to God's law; a fiery defender of the purity of my religion, even to the point of persecuting the church; a meticulous observer of everything set down in God's law Book. 7-9 The very credentials these people are waving around as something special, I'm tearing up and throwing out with the trash—along with everything else I used to take credit for. And why? Because of Christ. Yes, all the things I once thought were so important are gone from my life. Compared to the high privilege of knowing Christ Jesus as my Master, firsthand, everything I once thought I had going for me is insignificant—dog dung. I've dumped it all in the trash so that I could embrace Christ and be embraced by him. I didn't want some petty, inferior brand of righteousness that comes from keeping a list of rules when I could get the robust kind that comes from trusting Christ—God's righteousness. 10-11 I gave up all that inferior stuff so I could know Christ personally, experience his resurrection power, be a partner in his suffering, and go all the way with him to death itself. If there was any way to get in on the resurrection from the dead, I wanted to do it. 12-14 I'm not saying that I have this all together, that I have it made. But I am well on my way, reaching out for Christ, who has so wondrously reached out for me. Friends, don't get me wrong: By no means do I count myself an expert in all of this, but I've got my eye on the goal, where God is beckoning us onward—to Jesus. I'm off and running and I'm not turning back. 15-16 So let's keep focused on that goal, those of us who want everything God has for us. If any of you have something else in mind, something less than total commitment, God will clear your blurred vision—you'll see it yet! Now that we're on the right track, let's stay on it. 17-19 Stick with me, friends. Keep track of those you see running this same course, headed for this same goal. There are many out there taking other paths, choosing other goals, and trying to get you to go along with them. I've warned you of them many times; sadly, I'm having to do it again. All they want is easy street. They hate Christ's Cross. But easy street is a dead-*

end street. Those who live there make their bellies their gods; belches are their praise; all they can think of is their appetites. 20-21 But there's far more to life for us. We're citizens of high heaven! We're waiting the arrival of the Savior, the Master, Jesus Christ, who will transform our earthy bodies into glorious bodies like his own. He'll make us beautiful and whole with the same powerful skill by which he is putting everything as it should be, under and around him."

Chapter 4 (THE MESSAGE) *"My dear, dear friends! I love you so much. I do want the very best for you. You make me feel such joy, fill me with such pride. Don't waver. Stay on track, steady in God. 2 I urge Euodia and Syntyche to iron out their differences and make up. God doesn't want his children holding grudges. 3 And, oh, yes, Syzygus, since you're right there to help them work things out, do your best with them. These women worked for the Message hand in hand with Clement and me, and with the other veterans—worked as hard as any of us. Remember, their names are also in the Book of Life. 4-5 Celebrate God all day, every day. I mean, revel in him! Make it as clear as you can to all you meet that you're on their side, working with them and not against them. Help them see that the Master is about to arrive. He could show up any minute! 6-7 Don't fret or worry. Instead of worrying, pray. Let petitions and praises shape your worries into prayers, letting God know your concerns. Before you know it, a sense of God's wholeness, everything coming together for good, will come and settle you down. It's wonderful what happens when Christ displaces worry at the center of your life. 8-9 Summing it all up, friends, I'd say you'll do best by filling your minds and meditating on things true, noble, reputable, authentic, compelling, gracious—the best, not the worst; the beautiful, not the ugly; things to praise, not things to curse. Put into practice what you learned from me, what you heard and saw and realized. Do that, and God, who makes everything work together, will work you into his most excellent harmonies. 10-14 I'm glad in God, far happier than you would ever guess—happy that you're again showing such strong concern for me. Not that you ever quit praying and thinking about me. You just had no chance to show it. Actually, I don't have a sense of needing anything personally. I've learned by now to be quite content whatever my circumstances. I'm just as happy with little as with much, with much as with little. I've found the recipe for being happy whether full or hungry, hands full or hands empty. Whatever I have, wherever I am, I can make it through anything in the One who makes me who I am. I don't mean that your help didn't mean a lot to me—it did. It was a beautiful thing that you came alongside me in my troubles. 15-17 You Philippians well know, and you can be sure I'll never forget it, that when I first left Macedonia province, venturing out with the Message, not one church helped out in the give-and-take of this work except you. You were the only one. Even while I was in Thessalonica, you helped out—and not only once, but twice. Not that I'm looking for handouts, but I do want you to experience the blessing that issues from generosity.*

18-20 And now I have it all—and keep getting more! The gifts you sent with Epaphroditus were more than enough, like a sweet-smelling sacrifice roasting on the altar, filling the air with fragrance, pleasing God no end. You can be sure that God will take care of everything you need, his generosity exceeding even yours in the glory that pours from Jesus. Our God and Father abounds in glory that just pours out into eternity. Yes. 21-22 Give our regards to every follower of Jesus you meet. Our friends here say hello. All the Christians here, especially the believers who work in the palace of Caesar, want to be remembered to you. 23 Receive and experience the amazing grace of the Master, Jesus Christ, deep, deep within yourselves."

■■■ ■ ■◀◆▶■ ■ ■■■

"No one has seen God, but if we love one another, God lives in union with us, and His love is made perfect in us."
(I John 4:12 GNB)

Perfect Love Drives Out All Fear

◀ WEEK 30 ▶

Yes, *"we are sure that we live in union with God and that He lives in union with us, because He has given us His Spirit."* **(I John 4:13 GNB)** Submission to the Holy Spirit drives out all fear because He's living in us.

I started this day with thanksgiving and a prayer request for the manifest joy of the Lord to flow from my heart to each person I met today. *"The joy of the Lord is my strength..."* **(Nehemiah 8:10 NIV)** **The New American Standard (NAS)** version says it this way: *"... the joy of the Lord is your stronghold..."* **(Psalms 28:7 NIV)** also states *"...the Lord is my strength and my shield; my heart trusts in Him and I am helped..."*

Thank you, thank you Father, for Jesus! Thank you Jesus, for dying for each of us and for the gift of the Holy Spirit! Day by day, I must continue to die to self---which means giving up my selfish desires or no longer concentrating only on what I want. As I yield and submit to live in union with the Holy Spirit, I have great joy even through suffering and pain! This awareness comforts, heals and strengthens me to move forward in Jesus' Name. Amen! I want the Holy Spirit to lead and guide you too!

"If we obey God's commands, then we are sure that we know Him. If we say that we know Him, but do not obey His commands, we are liars and there is no truth in us. But if we obey His word, we are the ones whose love for God has really been made perfect. That is how we can be sure that we are in union with God: if we say that we remain in union with God, we should live just as Jesus Christ did." (**1 John 2:3-5 GNB**) As the popular movement says, we should ask 'What Would Jesus Do?' So, go to His Word, read it and put action to it!

The Message Bible (I John 2) says this about loving the world: *"...dear children: You know the Father from personal experience. You veterans know the One who started it all; and you newcomers... such vitality and strength! God's word is so steady in you. Your fellowship with God enables you to gain a victory over the Evil One. Don't love the world's ways. Don't love the world's goods. Love of the world squeezes out love for the Father. Practically everything that goes on in the world... wanting your own way, wanting everything for yourself, wanting to appear important... has nothing to do with the Father. It just isolates you from Him. The world and all its wanting, wanting, wanting is on the way out... but whoever does what God wants is set for eternity."* (Remember, that the Message Bible does not number verses, but in other versions, the above would have been in **verses 14-17**.) *"But thanks be to God! For in union with Christ we are always led by God as prisoners in Christ's victory procession."* (**II Corinthians 2:14 GNB**)

We are soldiers in the army of God -- veterans, as the Message Bible pointed out -- who will win the battle by putting our faith into action! Then, *"God uses us to make the knowledge about Christ spread everywhere like a sweet fragrance... We speak with sincerity in His presence, as servants of Christ."* (**II Corinthians 2:14b and 17 GNB**) *"Your life in Christ makes you strong, and His love comforts you. You have fellowship with the Spirit and you have kindness and compassion for one another."* (**Philippians 2:1 GNB**)

PRAYER

Holy Spirit, strengthen and lead us to serve and honor God. Lead us to "fall on our knees and openly proclaim Jesus Christ as Lord, to the glory of God the Father... " and "do everything without complaining or arguing, so that..." we are transformed "as God's perfect children..." (**Philippians 2:11-14 GNB**) *in Jesus' Name. Amen.*

MEDITATE ON THESE PASSAGES

Hebrews 10:14 (GNB) *"With one sacrifice, then, He has made perfect forever those who are purified from sin."*

Hebrews 10:1 (GNB) *"The Jewish Law is not a full, faithful model of the real things; it is only a faint outline of the good things to come. The same sacrifices offered year after year. How can the Law, then, by means of these sacrifices make perfect the people who come from God?"*

Hebrews 7:19 (GNB) *"For the Law of Moses could not make anything perfect... and now a better hope has been provided through which we can come near to God."*

Titus 2:14 (RSV) *"Jesus Christ gave Himself for us to redeem us from all iniquity and to purify for Himself a people of His own who are zealous for good deeds."*

■■■ ■ ■◀◆▶■ ■ ■■■

*"But if you look closely into the perfect law that sets people free,
and keep on paying attention to it and do not simply listen and forget it,
but put it into practice – you will be blessed by God in what you do."*
(James 1:25 GNB)

Look Closely Into the Perfect Law That Sets People Free

◀ WEEK 31 ▶

"Do not be deceived, my dear friends! Every good gift and every perfect present... comes down from God, the Creator of heavenly lights..." **(James 1:16-17 GNB)** Jesus also taught us to pray that it can be *"on earth as it is in Heaven..."* **(Matthew 6:10 NIV)** Look closely at the Lord's Prayer. Each one of us makes choices that, moment by moment, determine our life on earth. Oh yes, other people's choices affect us---but, each of us still has a choice over our individual responses.

"Remember this, my dear friends! Everyone must be quick to listen, but slow to speak and slow to become angry. Human anger does not achieve God's righteous purpose. So get rid of every filthy habit and all wicked conduct. Submit to God and accept the word that He plants in your hearts, which is able to save you. Do not deceive yourselves by just listening to His word; instead put it into practice... if you look closely into the perfect law that sets people free, and keep on paying attention to it and do not simply listen and forget it, but put it into practice---you will be blessed by God.." **(James 1:19-25 GNB)**

Do you want to be happy? Let's go back to **James 1:12-14**: *"Happy are those who remain faithful under trials, because when they succeed in passing such a test, they will receive as their reward the life which God has promised to those who love Him... we are tempted when we are drawn away and trapped by our own evil desires."*

When we make bad lifestyle choices, we are ignoring God and His instructions for us. We want to live our lives our way, not the way God says to live. I believe bad choices cause much of our anger. In the anger management classes I teach, I see and hear how bad choices cause lack of finances, the loss of friends, loved ones, self-respect and even health. In today's world there is a lot of anger. What is the root cause? It is disobedience to God's instructions, including failure to ask for help and dishonesty. The dishonesty includes lying to ourselves, even denial that we have such needs!

God is a good God and wants the best for each of us. The Bible reveals activities that are not good for us. One way or another, there are consequences and we pay for bad decisions. The simple answer is to let the Holy Spirit guide us daily by the Word of God. The Bible is our road map. Behavior choices and lifestyles outside of His guidelines lead to pain, fear, instability, and lack of vision. Even when legalized on earth, anything contrary to God's Word causes individual and social problems.

Let us choose today to *"closely... look into the perfect law that sets people free..."* **(James 1:25 GNB)** We need to be praying to be God's kind of perfect every day. We need prayer to allow the Holy Spirit to remove all imperfections. **(Ephesians 4:31 NIV)** The same Scripture in the Berean Bible even says: *"make"* us obey His *"perfect law."* Jesus is our assurance.

PRAYER

Father, thank You for transforming me into Your image through Jesus Christ with the

Holy Spirit's leading. Continue to illuminate my heart as I study Your Word. Let everything I do bring glory to You, in Jesus' Name. Amen.

MEDITATE ON THESE PASSAGES

1 Thessalonians 5:23 (Phillips) *"May the God of peace make you holy through and through. May you be kept in soul and mind and body in spotless integrity until the coming of our Lord Jesus Christ."*

II Peter 1:3 (NIV) *"His divine power has given us all we need for a godly life..."*

Hebrews 7:19 (KJV) *"For the Law made nothing perfect, but the bringing in of a better hope did; by the way which we draw nigh unto God."*

■■■　■　■◄◆►■　■　■■■

*"Those who love Your law have perfect security,
and there is nothing that can make them fall."*
(Psalms 119:165 GNB)

Perfect Security

◄ WEEK 32 ►

Lord, thank You that whether I'm reading in the New Testament or the Old, You are showing me the word 'perfect' on a daily basis. This is exciting and it encourages me. I hope it also encourages my readers, friends and family. It is so clear that You want perfect children. Though I continue aging, I am still Your child. Like Paul, I am dying daily to 'self', to the ways of my own self-determination so that I can live like You. Perhaps I made a false statement and didn't correct it. It could have been my pride rearing its ugly head, or failure to consider the possibility that I might be out of line. Lord, You may not like my behavior or attitude, but Your love for me never ends.

Our ministry, the Ark of Faith Foundation, with its **Matthew 25:35-36** service mandates to feed, clothe, visit, help and serve, helps me to keep my mind off myself. Holy Spirit, help us serve as Jesus served and to pray without ceasing! Only by sensitivity to the Holy Spirit and His feelings -- His whisper in our ears -- can we tune in to His 'voice frequency.' We can, indeed, hear His voice. We must open our ears to Him. We must hear---and obey quickly.

God alone can convict (persuade) us of sin in its various shapes and forms. I cannot lose my effectiveness by letting my pride (in any form) stop the flow of the Holy Spirit. Father, don't allow me to focus on projects and neglect what You need me to do. You have gifted me and I don't want to lose my 'edge' and usefulness. Holy Spirit, reveal to me and each of us when, where and what happens when we get us off course. *"...Any wrongdoing or disobedience must be faced in the power of Christ."* **(Philippians 4:13 GNB)**

Something or someone may seem perfect, but that may be only an illusion, a delusion. Only the Holy Spirit can give us the discernment that makes understanding possible regarding the extraordinary and the divine. At times, all humans feel divided, fractured or pulled in several different directions. We yearn for serenity and healing. The Holy Spirit will help us discover the way of healing from inside our pain if we just ask; get alone with Him, listen, and act. If we quit playing God and let the Spirit living in us be our Perfector, then our pain brings us closer and closer to God. We must ask for help and deliverance and then, recognize and receive it.

On the other hand, Satan wants us to become depressed. Don't become a victim of the devil's accusations! Satan is the accuser who wants us to focus on our wrongdoings or missteps. Instead, cry out for the revelation, strength and help of the Holy Spirit. *"Do not be anxious about anything, but in everything, by prayer and petition, with thanksgiving present your requests to God."* **(Philippians 4:6 NIV)**

Father God is our security. We must keep crying out and acknowledging our helplessness. This acknowledgement is the key. To me, **1 Peter 5:7** is a favorite verse. Here it is in three different Bible translations saying that the more challenges in life that we face with Him, the more we remember to:

- *"Cast all our cares upon Him, for He cares for us."* **(NKJ)**
- *"Give all your worries and cares to God for He cares about what happens to you."* **(NLT)**
- *"You can throw the whole weight of your anxieties upon Him for you are His personal concern."* **(Phillips)**

BECOMING PERFECT

Father God has such concern for us that He gave us Jesus, His only Son. *"....If we continue to live in Him, rooted and built up in Him, strengthened in faith... and overflowing with thankfulness... allowing no one to take us captive through hollow... deceptions... or human tradition... or basic principles of this world rather than on Christ... Christ is the head over every power and authority... having been raised with Him through... faith in the power of God... we were dead in sin... God made you alive with Christ... having disarmed the power and authorities... He made a public spectacle of them, triumphing over them by the cross."* **(Colossians 2:6-15 NIV)** That means He made each of us alive with Christ.

If we use Jesus as our example, we have our perfect security: our life in Him; our time alone with Father God.

PRAYER

Holy Spirit, open our spiritual eyes to the fact we are God's personal concern. He is our security! The more time we spend with Him, in prayer and His Word, the more knowledge we acquire. Help us, Holy Spirit, to become more sensitive to what brings Him pleasure! This I ask in the Name of Jesus. Amen.

MEDITATE ON THESE PASSAGES

Psalms 119:96 (GNB) *"I have learned that everything has limits; but Your commandment is perfect."*

Psalms 119:89-92 (GNB) *"Your word, O Lord, will last forever; it is eternal in heaven... If Your law had not been the source of my joy, I would have died from my sufferings."*

I Corinthians 1:8-9 (The Complete Jewish Bible, David Stern translation) *"He will enable you to hold out until the end and thus be blameless (perfect) on the day of our Lord Yeshua the Messiah – God is trustworthy; it was He who called you into fellowship with His Son, Yeshua, the Messiah, our Lord."*

1 Corinthians 1:8-9 (NIV) *"He will keep you strong to the end, so you will be blameless..."*

1 Corinthians 1:8-9 (GNB) *"He will also keep you firm to the end so that you will be faultless..."*

NOTES: _____

_____

_____

_____

_____

_____

_____

_____

_____

_____

_____

_____

_____

_____

_____

_____

_____

_____

_____

_____

_____

_____

_____

_____

BECOMING PERFECT

DIRECTION: _____

_____
_____
_____
_____
_____
_____
_____
_____
_____

PROGRESS: _____

_____
_____
_____
_____
_____
_____
_____
_____
_____

"When I lie down I go to sleep in peace; You alone, O Lord, keep me perfectly safe."
(Psalms 4:8 GNB)

Perfectly Safe

◄ WEEK 33 ►

Father God, You wanted a family to enjoy and for fellowship. You originally set that up in a beautiful garden. My 'garden of Eden' has a swimming pool surrounded by plants that I can tend. It is beautiful. I enjoy talking and singing praises to You while maintaining plants---watering them, pinching and pruning off the old so the new grows. I know Your presence and intimate relationship when I am in my personal garden of Eden.

In the world, You say we *"will know... persecutions, troubles, temptations and difficulties..."* **(II Corinthians 12:10 NIV)**. My 'garden' provides 'alone time' with You. That time provides regeneration, rest and renewal of my human spirit and body. Like Adam, each of us may make wrong choices; choices to please people and do what we choose versus choosing to be obedient to God's will and ways. Those wrong choices take us into places of unrest, unhappiness, even evil actions and thoughts. A spirit of fear may arise: "I should not have said [or done] that!" "We shouldn't have gone there!" "Save me Lord! I promise I won't [fill in the blank] anymore!" Or as Adam said in **Genesis 3:12-13**: *"...that woman You gave me made me..."* Those types of phrases are what some call 'pointing the finger', 'shifting blame' or the 'blame game'. Whatever it's called---it doesn't work. It changes nothing. It does not help you or those around you.

Confession and repentance do help. Those acts mean admitting that we own our part of the problem, 'dying to self' daily (like Paul) and facing the situation in *"all conditions by the power that Christ gives me."* **(Philippians 4:13 GNB)** Stop try to hide or cover-up evil. Like Paul did, we can all learn anywhere, at any time, to be content and peaceful in Jesus. **(Philippians 4:12 GNB)**

We are safe and know peace, love, joy, and happiness when we *"stand firm in our life in the Lord."* **(Philippians 4:1 GNB)** Jesus is looking for faithful partners who are overcomers.

BECOMING PERFECT

Here I quote from the Message Bible's introduction to Paul's letter to the **Hebrews**: *"It seems odd to have to say so, but too much religion is a bad thing. We can't get too much of God, too much faith and obedience or too much love and worship. But religion -- the well-intentioned efforts we make to 'get it all together' for God... for us -- we can get too much of that... our main and central action is everywhere and always what God has done, is doing, and will do for us... Jesus is the revelation of that action. Our main and central task is to live in responsive obedience to God's action revealed in Jesus. Our part in the action is the act of faith... more often than not we become impatiently self-important along the way and decide to improve matters with our own 'two cents worth'. We add on, we supplement, we embellish. But instead of improving on the purity and simplicity of Jesus, we dilute the purity and clutter the simplicity. We become fussily religious or anxiously active. We get in the way."*

In union with Christ, I can do all things and have all power and authority, such as is described in **(Luke 9:1-2 NIV)**: *"When Jesus had called the twelve disciples together, He gave them power and authority to drive out all demons and cure all diseases."* Only in union with Christ and by using the authority of His Name can there be Heaven *"on earth as it is in heaven."* **(Matthew 6:10 GNB)**

Perfecting means finishing and completing what God commands or tells us to do! Obedience is often learned through suffering. **(Job 36:15)** For us, Jesus set the example of handling such difficult learning experiences. The work *"is finished!"* **(John 19:30 GNB)** Our faith action is required moment by moment and is not a religious activity but is obedience to His will and purpose. *"We know that God makes all things work together for the good of those who love Him and are chosen to be a part of His plan."* **(Romans 8:28 NLT)**

PRAYER

Father, thank You for the gift of faith You gave so that, when I am weak, You can be strong in and for me. Jesus, help me live in Your Spirit and not in my emotions. Let my love for You come forth in obedience to the Father's will. In Your holy Name, I declare that You are with me, equipping me for every circumstance in this life. Amen.

MEDITATE ON THESE PASSAGES

Romans 13:9 (NIV) *"We are glad whenever we are weak but You are strong; and our prayer is for Your perfection."*

Hebrews 2:10 (NIV) *"In bringing many sons to glory, it was fitting that God, for whom and through whom everything exists, should make the author of their salvation perfect through suffering."*

Hebrews 10:1 (NIV) *"The law is only a shadow of the good things that are coming – not the realities themselves. For this reason it can never, by the same sacrifice repeated endlessly year after year, make perfect those who draw near to worship."*

■ ■ ■   ■   ■◀◆▶■   ■   ■ ■ ■

"Let us fix our eyes on Jesus, the Author and Perfector of our faith...
Consider Him who endured such opposition from sinful men,
so that you will not grow weary and lose heart..."
(Hebrews 12:2-3 NIV)

Above All: Pray

◀ *WEEK 34* ▶

Prayer is where each of us must go to keep our gaze fixed on Jesus. Once we have heard the voice of God we will not lose heart or grow weary. Paul says, *"Therefore we do not lose heart. Though outwardly we are wasting away, yet inwardly we are being renewed day by day. For our light and momentary troubles are achieving for us an eternal glory that far outweighs them all... So we fix our eyes, not on what is seen, but on what is unseen. For what is seen is temporary, but what is unseen is eternal."* **(II Corinthians 4:16-18 NIV)**

Many people come to the Ark distraught, questioning their abilities to walk by faith. Some are angry about situations or failed relations. Some weep, repenting of wrong lifestyles and bad decisions and choices. All of us face temptations daily. Bad things do happen to good people. However, bad things, abuse and rejection do not define who we are! We need to pray for more grace at the point of our need. We need to help others ask for grace at the point of their need. Here are four basic areas to consider when you stand between doubt and unbelief---and your faith walk.

1) God has a high calling for each of us. See how each of us must pursue the reality of His call. **(Philippians 4:13 GNB)** tells us to *"face the circumstances or situations ... in the power Christ gives ..."*

2) Each of us has hopes, aspirations and dreams in the day-to-day grind. *"Without a vision the people perish..."* **(Proverbs 29:18 KJV)**

3) Be real, true to the spiritual gifting given each of us by Father God. Demonstrate your true self in home, workplace and community. *"Now to each one the manifestation is given for common good... to one a message of wisdom, to another the message of knowledge by... the same Spirit..."* **(1 Corinthians 12:7-8 NIV)**

4) We must speak of what Jesus purchased for each of us by His death and acknowledge the benefits. *"...feed the church of God which he has purchased with His own blood..."* **(Acts 20:28 KJV)**

Prayer bridges the gap that stands between who we are today and what we are becoming. Spending more time alone praying (talking with and listening to God) moves us from where we are to where God desires us to be. Life is a journey and not an instantaneous event. We must take our promised land one step at a time. Each of us is given a measure of faith to bridge the gap between today and tomorrow. We must believe God's promise and take specific action that brings the promise into manifestation.

Many times in Scripture, we are told to pray without ceasing:

I Thessalonians 5:17-18 (NKJV) calls for us to *"...to pray on every occasion as the Spirit leads..."*

Ephesians 6:18 (GNB) says, *"Never stop praying, especially for others..."* and *"... in the power of the Spirit."*

Ephesians 5:20 (Contemporary English Version/CEV) tells us to *"...always use the name of Our Lord Jesus Christ to thank God the Father for everything."*

II Chronicles 7:14 (CEV) cites the Lord, *"If my own people will humbly pray and turn back to Me and stop sinning, then I will answer them from Heaven. I will forgive them and make their land fertile once again."*

We must not turn a blind eye to the natural circumstances. Rather, by faith in Father God and using the power and authority given us (the Name of Jesus Christ), we are to change circumstances to line up with His Word. Prayer changes us first, and then it changes things, as we obey and do what the Father instructs and commands. We show our faith by our action and part of our action is prayer. **(James 2:26 ISV)** says it well: *"In the same way, faith by itself, if it does not prove itself with actions, is dead."*

PRAYER

Father, I pray that, as Psalms 5:11-12 *says, "All who find safety in You will rejoice; they can always sing for joy. Protect those who love You; because of You they are happy. You bless those who obey You, Lord; Your love protects us like a shield." Lord Jesus, we need You and Your Holy Spirit, now. Amen.*

MEDITATE ON THESE PASSAGES

Psalms 5:1 (GNB) *"Listen to my words, O Lord, and hear my sighs. Listen to my cry for help, my God and King!"*

Psalms 5:2 (GNB) *"I pray to You, O Lord; You hear my voice in the morning; at sunrise I offer my prayer and wait for your answer."*

Psalms 100:4 (KJV) *"Enter His gates with thanksgiving; go into His courts with praise."*

1 Peter 4:10 (CEV) *"Each of you have been blessed with one of God's many wonderful gifts to be used in the service of others. So use your gift well."*

Romans 8:26 (NKJV) *"Likewise the Spirit also helps in our weakness. For we do not know what we should pray for as we ought, but the Spirit Himself makes intercession for us with groanings which cannot be uttered."*

*"Even before the world was made, God had already chosen us to be His through our
union with Christ, so that we would be holy and without fault."*
(Ephesians 1:4 GNB)

Chosen to Be Holy and Without Fault

◄ WEEK 35 ►

Without fault means perfect. **(Proverbs 25:4 GNB)** says *"Take the impurities out of
silver and the artist can produce a thing of beauty."* The Potter (God, as Artist) is taking
the imperfections out of all who are willing to be changed or formed into a "thing" of
beauty. (God even uses His sense of humor when He calls a wife a good "thing" instead
of a person in **(Proverbs 18:22 GNB)**. Are we making excuses when we say, "We're only
human…"? Are we trying to escape our responsibilities and excuse our selfish, self-
centered or impatient ways?

To gain inner peace we need to face each newly discovered imperfection *"in the power of
Christ."* **(Philippians 4:13 GNB)** We need to stop denying or fighting the truth about our
human selves when that self is exposed. In weakness we can discover strength. When
we *"...set our minds on what the Spirit desires… the mind controlled by the Spirit is life and
peace..."* **(Romans 8:5-6 GNB)** Sometimes, to get from where we are, we must let go of the
old and familiar or the unhealthy to allow the Holy Spirit to renew our minds and make
them like the mind of Christ. We must *"...be transformed by the renewing of our mind...to
His good, pleasing and perfect will."* **(Romans 12:2 NIV)** *"For those God foreknew, He also
predestined to be conformed to the likeness of His Son..."* **(Romans 8:29 NIV)**

We were chosen and so we need a relentless spirit to pursue the things of God. We must
"press toward the goal for the prize of the upward call of God in Christ Jesus." **(Philippians
3:14 NIV)** Each of us must allow the Holy Spirit to reveal all imperfections in us and
work them out. In **II Corinthians 13:5**, the **Message Bible** says, *"Test yourselves to make
sure you are solid in faith. Don't drift along taking everything for granted. Give yourselves
regular checkups… firsthand evidence, not more hearsay, that Jesus Christ is in you. Test it*

out. If you fail the test, do something about it." We must stop using the excuse that only Jesus was (is) perfect. He called us to be like Him and do what He did!

God not only wants the minds of His chosen children to be transformed at the time of their repentance, but also to be renewed completely in an ongoing, every day transformation. "*So then, my friends, because of God's great mercy to us I appeal to you: Offer yourselves as a living sacrifice… dedicated to His services and pleasing to Him. Do not conform yourselves to the standards of this world, but let God transform you inwardly… so you will be able to know the will of God---what is good and is pleasing to Him and is perfect.*" **(Romans 12:1-2 GNB)** "*No one has seen God at any time; if we love one another, God abides in us and His love is perfected in us. By this we know that we abide in Him, and He in us, because He has given us His Spirit.*" **(1 John 4:12-13 NIV)**

Friends, we were chosen to love and be loved. Satan wants to deceive and delude our minds to believe that we are unloved and unlovely. That is the big lie.

We must not believe that lie. We were chosen to love our neighbor as ourselves and to fellowship with God and each other. We, as believers, should continually ask God to purify our minds and wash out all bad thoughts and vain imaginations toward God and others. We must allow Him to cleanse and strengthen our minds according to His will and ways. This assures us that we will live fully in accordance with the eternal will of God.

PRAYER

Father, the Greek word teleios literally means "fully complete". In (Matthew 5:48 NKJV) the word teleios was the original from which the translation 'perfect' was used to quote Jesus. In English, it says, "Therefore be ye perfect as your heavenly Father is perfect." My prayer is that each one of us and each member of our families may be made fully complete (perfect) by the Holy Spirit, in Jesus' Name and for Your Glory. Amen.

MEDITATE ON THESE PASSAGES

II Corinthians 11:3 (NKJV) "*But I fear lest somehow, as the serpent deceived Eve by his craftiness, your thoughts would be corrupted from the simplicity and the purity toward Christ's…*"

Matthew 5:48 (NKJV) *"Therefore be ye perfect as your heavenly Father is perfect."*

Psalms 4:3 (GNB) *"Remember that the Lord has chosen the righteous for his own, and he hears me when I call to him."*

■■■　■　■◄◆►■　■　■■■

*"Therefore, since we are surrounded by such a great cloud of witnesses,
let us throw off everything that hinders and the sin that so easily entangles,
and let us run with perseverance the race marked out for us.
Let us fix our eyes on Jesus, the author and perfector of our faith..."*
(Hebrews 12:1-2 NIV)

Jesus, Perfector of Our Faith

◄ WEEK 36 ►

Having read the above introductory passage of **Hebrews 12**, I continued on to **verse 3** where we are told not "to grow weary and lose heart." Also, (**Proverbs 3:11-12 NLT**) says, *"My son, do not make light of the Lord's discipline, and do not lose heart when He rebukes you. Because the Lord disciplines those He loves, and He punishes everyone He accepts as a son."*

At times we are told to endure hardship---and that could be discipline. *"...God disciplines us for our good that we may share in His holiness..."* (**Hebrews 12:10b NIV**) In **verse 13**, the Scripture points out a form of training for healing to manifest itself while we experience something painful. We are told to *"...make every effort to live in peace with all men and to be holy..."* for *"without holiness no one will see the Lord."* Each of us must come to God alone because He is *"the judge of all men... righteous men made perfect..."* (**Hebrews 12:14b-23b NIV**)

Jesus' blood ushers in the new covenant. You can see this as you keep reading in the same Scripture: *"Therefore, since we are receiving a kingdom that cannot be shaken, let us be thankful, and so worship God acceptably with reverence and awe, for our God is a*

106

consuming fire." **(Hebrews 12:28-29 NIV)**

Don't forget that we remain God's children---even as adults. The purpose of discipline is to show children that unhealthy or destructive behavior has consequences. While children are growing up, some parents may have been absent so those children show a lack of discipline even into adulthood. Sometimes the discipline may have been too harsh or abusive and those children show a resistance to discipline---even rebellion against it. Discipline can also be given inconsistently and show up later in unhealthy confusion and double-mindedness.

Beating or face slapping are often angry reactions and are incorrect ways to discipline. Yet, **(Proverbs 13:24 NIV)** reminds us that: *"who spares the rod hates his son, but he who loves him is careful to discipline him."* My life experience reveals that today's children and many, many teens are angry and rebellious. They often act out to get various attention or response. Some research says this is primarily due to parents having so little time to be present with them. It is certainly true as seen from my experience as a spiritual counselor.

Discipline means training or correction. Train children in Godly character and they will have the knowledge and skill to handle life's circumstances. Don't give up when they don't get it right the first time, persist. Consistently, respectfully show them how to choose self-control. Allow them to 'suffer' consequences when they make ungodly choices. Coach them to include gratitude in celebrating when they make godly choices. Whom you love, you discipline. Your Father God does the same with you. These training, coaching, disciplining principles are found throughout Scriptures like Hebrews 12, Proverbs 3, Job 5, Luke 9 and many more.

Healthy discipline can and does exist. It comes out of love, not rage! It should be firm and appropriate to the situation, avoiding shame or blame. It should be consistent---with love clearly communicated! God exemplifies the right way to correct, chasten or discipline. **(Proverbs 13:1-18 NIV)** states, *"A wise son heeds his father's instruction, but a mocker does not listen to rebuke... he who ignores discipline comes to poverty and shame, but whoever heeds correction is honored."*

As Christians, we want to accept and give discipline in love. Can you join me in this prayer?

BECOMING PERFECT

PRAYER

Lord, help us return to Your will and ways so that, as Hebrews 12:23 states, we can be "made perfect." I ask the Holy Spirit's help both to hear and obey, and have the ability to make right choices. Indeed, Lord, there is no other way but to trust and obey You. Spiritual growth and recovery are like a race that each one of us runs and must finish to reach our goals of perfection in Jesus. Please help us to discipline our children in the way that You discipline us. I ask this in Jesus' Name, Amen.

MEDITATE ON THESE PASSAGES

II Timothy 1:12 (Phillips) *"I know the One in whom I have placed my confidence, and I am perfectly certain that the work He has committed to me is safe in His hands until that Day."*

Hebrews 9:11 (GNB) *"Christ has already come as the High Priest of the good things that are already here. The tent in which He serves is greater and more perfect... not made by human hands, that is, it is not a part of this created world."*

Hebrews 9:8-9 (GNB) *"The Holy Spirit clearly teaches... the way into the Most Holy Place... it means the offerings and animal sacrifices presented to God cannot make the worshipper's heart perfect..."*

Hebrews 12:1-11 (NET) *"My son, do not scorn the Lord's discipline or give up when he corrects you. For the Lord disciplines the one he loves and chastises every son he accepts. Endure your suffering as discipline; God is treating you as sons... But if you do not experience discipline, something all sons have shared in, then you are illegitimate and are not sons. Besides, we have experienced discipline from our earthly fathers and we respected them... For they disciplined us for a little while as seemed good to them, but He does so for our benefit, that we may share His holiness. Now all discipline seems painful at the time, not joyful. But later it produces the fruit of peace and righteousness for those trained by it."*

NOTES: _____

_____

_____

_____

_____

_____

_____

_____

_____

_____

_____

_____

_____

_____

_____

_____

_____

_____

_____

_____

_____

_____

_____

_____

BECOMING PERFECT

DIRECTION: _____

_____
_____
_____
_____
_____
_____
_____
_____
_____
_____

PROGRESS: _____

_____
_____
_____
_____
_____
_____
_____
_____
_____

"This God – how perfect are His deeds! How dependable His words! He is like a shield for all who seek His protection. The Lord alone is God; God alone is our defense."
(Psalms 18:30-31 GNB)

How Dependable His Words

◄ WEEK 37 ►

If we want to be happy, we need to submit to the will and ways of the Holy Spirit and Father God, and heed their warnings like Jesus did. The dependable words and correction of the Triune God will supply the joy we seek, as seen in the two scriptural examples below:

"The law of the Lord is perfect; it gives new strength. The commands of the Lord are trustworthy, giving wisdom to those who lack it. The laws of the Lord are right and those who obey them are happy." **(Psalms 19:7-8 GNB)**

"Because the Lord is righteous and good, He teaches sinners the path they should follow. He leads the humble in the right way and teaches them His will. With faithfulness and love He leads all who keep His covenant and obey His commands." **(Psalms 25:8-10 GNB)**

Our ancestors who followed Moses ate and drank from the spiritual rock; *"...that rock was Christ Himself..."* The Scripture continues *"...to warn us not to desire evil things... worship idols... have orgies of drinking and sex... sexual immorality... put the Lord to the test... complain..."* We know the character of God: *"The Lord is faithful to His promises; He is merciful in all His acts. He helps those who are in trouble; He lifts those who have fallen."* Yes readers, *"God keeps His promise and will not allow you to be tested beyond your power to remain firm; at the time you are put to the test, He will give... strength to endure and... provide ...a way out."* **(I Corinthians 10:1-14 GNB)**

Father God does not want us just to endure our imperfections, but to renew our minds to the mind of Christ in order to bring about the necessary life changes. *"All of us have sinned and fallen short of the glory of God..."* **(Romans 3:23 KJV)** That is why from the beginning *"He said, let us make man in our own image..."* (**Genesis 1:26 KJV**) When the man who the Father created disobeyed and ate the fruit of the forbidden tree, God knew His people needed a Savior. With all of our humanity, inadequacies, helplessness, lack of self-control, and failures, God knew we would need restoration so He provided the Holy Spirit to live in each of us.

We know when we choose to do wrong. Perhaps we watered the soil of our lives with alcohol or fertilized it with pornography or grew it with thoughts of envy or jealousy. We chose the path that caused (and may still cause) us to suffer. At the time, we may not have understood totally the consequences of those bad decisions and choices. Still, most of us have seen others who appear to be off-balance, broken, twisted or torn apart---even if we haven't recognized it in ourselves.

God's Word warns and urges us to *"come out from among them..."* (**II Corinthians 6:17 KJV**) It's clear that we are to leave the people and places of sin and idol worship, to leave that place and its struggle behind and instead, seek the redemption of Christ Jesus! We are told to become overcomers, not just survivors. So, first, we must acknowledge our self-indulgence, and face our imperfections *"in the power of Christ..."* (**Philippians 4:13 GNB**) We are to use the authority given us in Jesus' Name.

PRAYER

Holy Spirit, reveal what help each one of us needs to overcome our imperfections. Lead us day by day into victory. I want to start today to rely on You more, in Jesus' Name. Amen.

MEDITATE ON THESE PASSAGES

Hebrews 6:1-3 (GNB) *"Let us go forward then, to mature teaching and leave behind us the first lessons of the Christian message... turn away from useless works..."*

I Chronicles 22:19 (AMPC) *"Set your mind and heart to seek (inquire of and require as your vital necessity) the Lord your God..."*

Psalms 19:13 (GNB) *"Keep me safe, also, from willful sins; don't let them rule over me. Then I shall be perfect and free from the evil of sin."*

Psalms 25:4-5 (GNB) *"Teach me Your ways, O Lord, make them known to me. Teach me to live according to Your truth, for You are my God, who saves me. I will always trust in You."*

■ ■ ■   ■   ■◀◆▶■   ■   ■ ■ ■

"...who may enter His holy temple? Those who are pure in act and thought,
who do not worship idols or make false promises."
(Psalms 24:3b-4 GNB)

Pure In Act and Thought

◀ *WEEK 38* ▶

"...Christ came as high priest of the good things that are already here, He went through the
greater and more perfect tabernacle that is not man-made, that is to say, it is not a part of
this creation. He did not enter by means of the blood of goats and calves, but He entered
the Most Holy Place once for all by His own blood, having obtained eternal redemption."
(Hebrews 9:11-12 NIV) Ceremonial, outward appearances of cleanliness do nothing,
but the blood of Christ cleanses our consciences and the acts that would otherwise lead
to death. Why? It was *"So that we may... serve the living God!"* **(Hebrews 9:13b-14**
NIV) It all means that *"...the offerings and animal sacrifices presented to God cannot*
make the worshipper's heart perfect." **(Hebrews 9:9b GNB)**

God wants group worship. *"You have come to the joyful gathering of God's firstborn,*
whose names are written in heaven. You have come to God, who is judge of all people, and
to the spirits of good people made perfect." **(Hebrews 12:23 GNB)**

Jesus wants us to be in a church. How I love and enjoy my church family and our various
weekly fellowships. Do you? **(Hebrews 12:25-29 GNB)** continues: *"Be careful then, and*
do not refuse to hear him who speaks. Those who refused to hear the one who gave the divine
message on earth did not escape. How much less shall we escape then, if we turn away from
the One who speaks from heaven! ...Let us be grateful and worship God in a way that will
please Him, with reverence and awe; because our God is indeed a destroying fire."

God is a refining fire. The Perfector is making us whole---removing all spot and wrinkle. God is practical. He knows his training, refining, discipline is tough. He knows
we accept tough things better together, supporting each other. *"Let us, then, always of-*
fer praise to God as our sacrifice through Jesus, which is the offering presented by lips that

confess Him as Lord. Do not forget to do good and to help one another, because these are the sacrifices that please God." (**Hebrews 13:15-16 GNB**) *"Religion that God our Father accepts as pure and faultless is this: to look after orphans and widows in their distress and to keep oneself from being polluted by the world."* (**James 1:27 NIV**)

Let us end this chapter with (**II Peter 1:5-7 GNB**): *"For this very reason"* we want to do our very *"...best to add goodness to our faith... to goodness add knowledge... to knowledge add self-control... to self-control add endurance... to endurance add godliness... to godliness add Christian affection... to Christian affection add love."* Then we shall be pure in act and thought and live in peace and fellowship with Father God, Jesus Christ, the Holy Spirit, and each other---so our joy will be complete.

PRAYER

Father, I submit every area of my life to You. Cleanse my heart and mind as You teach me Your ways. Help me to build and maintain purity and holiness as I give to and receive from my fellowship, my church. I desire to walk with You and experience every blessing You have for me in Jesus Christ. Amen.

MEDITATE ON THESE PASSAGES

James 2:21-22 (GNB) *"How was our ancestor Abraham put right with God? ...through his actions ...can't you see? His faith and actions worked together; his faith was made perfect through his action."*

James 3:17 (GNB) *"But the wisdom from above is pure first of all; it is also peaceful, gentle and friendly; it is full of compassion and produces a harvest of good deeds; it is free from prejudice and hypocrisy."*

Deuteronomy 32:4 (GNB) *"The Lord is your mighty defender, perfect and just in all His ways; Your God is faithful; and He does what is right and fair."*

James 1:22-25 (GNB) *"Do not deceive yourselves by just listening to His word; instead put it into practice... look closely into the perfect law that sets people free... do not simply listen ... then forget... but put it into practice and you will be blessed of God."*

∎∎∎ ∎ ◗◀◆▶◖ ∎ ∎∎∎

"...they follow the Lamb wherever He goes. They have been redeemed from the rest of the human race...they have never been known to tell lies; they are faultless."
(Revelation 14:4-5 CEV)

They Are Faultless

◀ WEEK 39 ▶

Faultless (adj.) - Perfect, flawless, without fault, free of error, impeccable, accurate, precise, exact, correct, exemplary... *~Roget's Thesaurus*

We are told to renew our minds to the mind of Christ (**Romans 12:2 NIV**). Paul learned to *"die daily"* to the ways of the self---and so must I! How about you?

(**Deuteronomy 32:4 GNB**) tells us, *"The Lord is your mighty defender, perfect and just in all His ways... faithful and true; He does what is right and fair."* If we renew our minds to the mind of Christ, then we, too, will be faultless (perfect). It is our choice. It is not easy, but Christ and the Holy Spirit promise us it will be worth it. *"All of us... are being transformed from glory to glory into His very image by the Lord who is the Spirit."* (**II Corinthians 3:18 NAB**)

"The Lord is the Spirit, and where the Spirit of the Lord is, there is freedom... We repudiate shameful, underhanded practices. We do not resort to trickery or falsify the word of God. We proclaim the truth openly... we are afflicted in every way possible, but we are not crushed; full of doubts, we never despair. We are persecuted but never abandoned; we are struck down but never destroyed... we make it our aim to please Him... The lives of all of us are to be revealed before the tribunal so that each one may receive his recompense, good or bad, according to his life in the body." (**II Corinthians 3:17-6:10 NAB**)

We may fall down or stray. We often look on external appearances or have self-centered reasoning. *"God is the reason... when we are brought back to our senses... it is the love of Christ impelling us... all this has been done by God, who has reconciled us to Himself through Christ and given us the ministry of reconciliation... not counting men's transgres-*

sion against them… For our sakes, God made Him who did not know sin to be sin, so that in Him we might become the very holiness of God." **(II Corinthians 4:13-21 NAB)**

Father God, I thank You for Your Son Jesus and for calling us to be like Him: pure, holy and perfect. We are called to be the temple of God in Christ Jesus. We are welcomed! We are made His sons and daughters, when we obey and separate ourselves from unbelievers who are living worldly lifestyles. We are exhorted to *"purify ourselves from every defilement of flesh and spirit, and in the fear of God strive to fulfill our consecration perfectly."* **(II Corinthians 6-7:1 NAB)**

Jesus came to serve as the Father had shown and told Him--- He did what God taught Him to do with Word and deed. *"He does not neglect the poor or ignore their suffering... but answers when they call for help."* **(Psalms 22:24 GNB)** However, go back and read the previous **verses 22-23**, *"I will tell my people what you have done; I will praise you in their assembly... Praise him you servants of the Lord!"* It wasn't just Jesus Who came to serve. We are called to serve as Jesus did. We are commanded to go and tell the good news and to love others -- in crowds, assemblies or one-on-one -- wherever there is need. **The Message Bible** states in **Colossians 3:22**, *"...servants, do what you're told by your earthly masters, and don't just do the minimum that will get you by. Do your best."* Don't just do the minimum? That was an eye opener when I read it. Doing my best means giving my all, just like my Example Jesus did. Jesus gave it all.

Would you join me in this prayer?

PRAYER

Thank you, Jesus, for restoring the Holy Spirit to each of us! We need Your strength, help and guidance as we strive to become faultless. Indeed, "create a pure heart in me, O God, and put a new and loyal spirit in me..." **(Psalms 51:10 GNB)** *and in each one who reads this! I ask in Your holy Name. Amen*

MEDITATE ON THESE PASSAGES

Matthew 19:21 (NIV) *"Jesus answered, If you want to be perfect, go, sell your possessions and give to the poor and you will have treasure in heaven. Then come, follow me."*

Matthew 5:46-48 (GNB) *"Why should God reward you if you love only the people who love you? If you speak only to your friends, have you done anything out of the ordinary? Even the pagans do that! You must be perfect – just as your Father in heaven is perfect."*

I John 2:5 (KJV) *"But whosoever keepeth His Word, on him verily is the love of God perfected. Hereby know we that we are in Him."*

▪▪▪ ▪ ▪◀◆▶▪ ▪ ▪▪▪

"Do not conform yourselves to the standards of this world, but let God transform you inwardly by a complete change of your mind. Then you will be able to know the will of God – what is good and is pleasing to Him and is perfect."
(Romans 12:2 GNB)

The Will of God Is Good… Pleasing… Perfect

◀ WEEK 40 ▶

How often do we pray "Thy will, not mine"? Or, "Father, Your will be done" in this situation or circumstance? "Show me Your way"? "I want to please You"? I even say, "Father, I want to hear You say, 'Well done, my good and faithful servant'…" Remember, our actions speak louder than words.

Today, in my lectionary schedule of Scripture readings, I saw something I've read, but missed for years: His will is perfect! **(Romans 12:2 NLT)** Father, thank you again for this study. You are the Perfector. You are removing my blinders.

Too often, I have chosen the world's ways. I have repeated over and over the phrase, "Nobody is perfect." Then, I saw today what that means. I was holding on to self-indulgent ways versus completing the changes in my mind necessary to be "good… pleasing… perfect." By saying 'Nobody is perfect,' I am reaping what I sow: imperfection! Those words are excuses and are less than what is pleasing to God. It's like giving second best, yet all the while I am praying, "Thy will be done."

Wow! That's double-minded---and a double-minded person does not get what he or she wants. (Oh, forgive me, Lord! Holy Spirit, help me to completely change my mind inwardly, in Jesus' Name. Amen.)

As I wrote this chapter, we were nearing the Advent season, the time of year when we prepare to celebrate the birth of Jesus. Since my first book *Alone with God at Christmas,* I have known that Father God meant for us to carry Christmas in our hearts every single day. Still, I know this Advent season is special as the time to remember why we celebrate our Savior's birth. Still, I need the Holy Spirit's help to do it the (**Romans 12:1-13 GNB**) way: *"So then, my friends, because of God's great mercy to us I appeal to you: offer your-selves as a living sacrifice to God, dedicated to His service and pleasing to Him. This is true worship that you should offer."* We must all do this. So, Father, help us to share our belongings with needy fellow Christians and open our homes to strangers. We are told to hate what is evil (**verse 9**) and hold on firmly to what is good. The same Scripture in **verse 11** says: *"We are to serve the Lord with a heart full of devotion."*

What has Christmas become? The shopping and gift-giving starts long before the date we celebrate Jesus' birth. Often, the season even becomes a debt-builder. Pressures, greed and selfish desires frequently instigate angry outbursts. Is this what makes us perfect? Is thinking this way moving us to our goal to be like Him?

At Christmas, and all through the year, can we adopt the recommendations continuing in (**Romans 12:14-21 GNB**)? They are to: *"...ask God to bless those who persecute us – yes, ask Him not to curse them."* This would be a great gift and service! Then we could *"...be happy with those who are happy, weep with those who weep. Have the same concern for everyone. Do not be proud, but accept humble duties. Do not think of yourselves as wise ...do what everyone considers to be good. Do everything possible on our part, to live in peace with everybody."* Finally, *"Do not let evil defeat you; instead, conquer evil with good."* These Scriptures mean for us to do these things all the time, not just at Christ-mas. They didn't even hold Christmas celebrations in the days the Scriptures were writ-ten! These principles were intended to be daily guidance all through the years.

PRAYER

Help each of us, Holy Spirit, to "...serve the Lord with a heart full of devotion. Let your hope keep us joyful ...patient in our troubles, and praying at all times." (Romans 12:

11-12 GNB) *Let this be our daily effort, in Jesus' Name. Amen.*

MEDITATE ON THESE PASSAGES

II Samuel 22:33-34 (KJV) *"God is my strength and power and he maketh my way perfect. He maketh my feet like hinds feet; and setteth me upon high places."*

Psalms 24:33-4 (GNB) *"...Who may enter His holy Temple? Those who are pure in act and in thought, who do not worship idols or make false promises."*

Philippians 4:8 (NAB) *"Finally, my brothers, your thoughts should be wholly directed to all that is true, all that deserves respect, all that is honest, pure, admirable, decent, virtuous or worthy of praise."*

II Corinthians 3:18 (GNB) *"And we, who with unveiled faces all reflect the Lord's glory, are being transformed into His likeness with ever-increasing glory, which comes from the Lord, who is the Spirit."*

I Corinthians 13:9-10 (GNB) *"For our gifts of knowledge and inspired messages are only partial but when what is perfect comes, then what is partial will disappear."*

NOTES: _____

_____

_____

_____

_____

_____

_____

_____

_____

NOTES: _____

_____

_____

_____

_____

_____

_____

_____

_____

_____

_____

_____

_____

_____

_____

_____

_____

_____

_____

_____

DIRECTION: _____

_____

_____

_____

_____

_____

_____

_____

_____

_____

_____

_____

PROGRESS: _____

_____

_____

_____

_____

_____

_____

_____

_____

_____

*"Thou wilt keep him in perfect peace,
whose mind is stayed on thee, because he trusteth in thee."*
(Isaiah 26:3 KJV)

Wait For Holy Spirit Guidance

◄ WEEK 41 ►

Today, Corrie ten Boom reminded me to make my plans while in prayer. None of us need to recklessly rush ahead of God. In her book Each New Day, her final plea was, "Lord, keep us from rash actions, no matter how right they seem at the time."

To make good decisions and plans, we need peace of mind. As this hit me, I started searching different translations of **Isaiah 26:3**:

NIV *"You will keep in perfect peace him whose mind is steadfast, because he trusts in You!"*

RSV *"Those of steadfast mind You keep in peace---in peace because they trust in You."*

Jewish *"A person whose desire rests on You---You preserve in perfect peace, because he trusts in You."*

Amplified *"You will guard him and keep him in perfect and constant peace whose mind (both its inclinations and its character) is stayed on You, because he commits himself to You, leans on You, and hopes confidently in You."*

GNB *"You Lord, give perfect peace to those who keep their purpose firm and put their trust in You."*

The Webster's dictionary defines the adjective steadfast as: firm, resolute. Its verb translation is: to make or become steady. The word stay means: to remain, hold out or persevere. Its verb translation is: to halt, stop, pause, linger; suspend; delay, prop up; support.

Prayer then, is when we are asking, waiting before (and with) the Lord; holding out until the Holy Spirit's guidance is clear and we confidently know and trust the Father's support for, and His will about our plans. This absolutely means we must stop, linger, pause, and listen! If a household is full of noise -- things like talking, television and videos, rage and anger -- there is little or no peace. There is also nobody doing any actual or focused listening!

We must get alone with God! Do it in the same way that our Father is committed to focusing on each of us. Like Corrie ten Boom wrote that she did, we need to pray: "Lord, keep us from rash actions..." in the heat of this moment!

The Lord knows our plight and our discomfort when we are in adversity. At those times we need to halt, linger and cry out: *"O, Lord, unto You do I lift up my soul. O my God, I trust in thee: let me not be ashamed, let not my enemies triumph over me."* **(Psalms 25:1-2 KJV)**

As we pause, delay and get propped up by the Holy Spirit, we must accept His peace in the midst of the storm, the real trouble. The Comforter will then lead us and guide us *"through the valley of the shadow of death..."* **(Psalms 23: 4 KJV)** Do you see? We do get through. The Peace Giver is with us all the way; we need only to commit to Him so we can hear direction clearly.

As the Jewish Bible's translation of our **Isaiah 26:3** Scripture reminds us, we must get our desire on Him -- rather than on things or people -- and He will preserve each of us.

PRAYER

Our trust must be in You, Lord Jesus, and not in people. We must incline our ears to You for our daily journey and support. Lord, I am confident and I trust in You. Let me rejoice in this learning experience we are given through You, Christ Jesus! Amen

MEDITATE ON THESE PASSAGES

Hebrews 11:40 (GNB) *"... because God had decided on an even better plan for us. His purpose was that only in company with us would they be made perfect."*
I Peter 1:7 (KJV) *"That the trial of your faith being much more precious than of gold that*

perisheth, though it be tried with fire, might be found unto praise and honor and glory at the appearing of Jesus Christ."

Acts 11:21, 23 (NLT) *"The Lord's hand was with them, and a great number of people believed and turned to the Lord... when he arrived and saw the evidence of the grace of God, he was glad and encouraged them all to remain true to the Lord with all their hearts."*

James 1:4 (GNB) *"Make sure that your endurance carries you all the way without failing, so that you may be perfect and complete.*

■■■ ■ ◼◀◆▶◼ ■ ■■■

"Since this is true, how much more is accomplished by the blood of Christ! Through the eternal Spirit, He offered Himself as a perfect sacrifice to God."
(Hebrews 9:14 GNB)

Blood of Christ---a Perfect Sacrifice to God

◄ WEEK 42 ►

"The offerings and animal sacrifices presented to God cannot make the worshipper's heart perfect..." **(Hebrews 9:9 GNB)** *"...For this reason, Christ is the one who arranges a new covenant, so that those who have been called by God may receive the eternal blessings..."* **(Hebrews 9:15 GNB)**

"Christ has already come as the High Priest of the good things that are already here. The tent in which He serves is greater and more perfect... He took His own blood and obtained eternal salvation for us... Since this is true, how much more is accomplished by the blood of Christ! Through the eternal Spirit, He offered Himself as a perfect sacrifice to God. His blood will purify our consciences from useless rituals so that we may serve the living God." **(Hebrew 9:11-14 GNB)**

God made the first man, Adam, to *"tend the garden..."* **(Genesis 2:15 NLT)** He created him to cultivate it and guard it. He gave human beings duties and responsibilities. *"God said... they will be like us and resemble us. He created them male and female, blessed* *them and said, "Have many children... your descendants will live all over the earth... I am putting you in charge..."* (**Genesis 1:26-28 NIV**)

All was good in the beginning; until a wrong choice was made. Like many of us today, Adam knew he disobeyed. However, he blamed Eve---after he blamed God. That's right! He said, "It was the woman You gave me who made me..." (Genesis 3:12, NLT) Eve then blamed the serpent. Today, wrong choices are still being made. Of course, we know wrong from right and yet, we still make excuses, blaming others, even God. Our lack of obedience to God's Word shows up in many ways. Two men cannot produce any descendants; neither can two women. We no longer tend or care for fish, birds and animals as God directed. Many people are too lazy to work His fields or to train up a child "in the way he should go..." (Proverbs 22:6, NKJV) The following Scriptures are just a few examples of prophecy and training to pray, hear and obey God's Word, His instructions:

God says He desires that none should perish. He does *"not want any of these little ones to be lost..."* (**Matthew 18:14 GNB**)

Jesus says, "I must preach the good news.... that is what God sent me to do." (**Luke 4:43 GNB**)

I Peter 1:12 (GNB) reminds us that God sends "prophets... messengers who will announce the good news by the power of the Holy Spirit."

In the Old Testament, Jeremiah was used to show and tell us that nothing is too difficult for God. From the very beginning there have been messengers and prophets to tell good news. *"I am the Lord...is anything too difficult for me...?"* (**Jeremiah 32:27 NIV**)

The blood of Jesus cleanses all of us. Which sin is the greatest and which is worst? I love **Revelation 21:8** below! God used that to bring me to my knees. Except for the grace of God, the coward inside of me would have stubbornly refused to spread the good news. Yes, I was surprised to find that a coward is at the top of the 'sinner list.' *"But cowards, traitors, perverts, murderers, the immoral, those who practice magic, those who worship idols, and all liars - the place for them is the lake burning with fire and sulphur which is the second death."* (**Revelation 21:8 GNB**)

Each of us has choices. If the Spirit of God transforms us from within, we will exhibit divine characteristics. We are not the 'accuser of our brothers'. That's Satan. *"...but we should be warning every man, and teaching every man in all wisdom; that we may present every man perfect in Christ Jesus."* (**Colossians 1:28 NKJV**)

PRAYER

Thank You, Father, for victory through Jesus' shed blood. This act set in motion the Holy Spirit's life within us, to lead and guide us to be messengers of this good news so that no child should be lost. Because I am Your child, strengthen me with more anointing to fulfill Your purpose today and every day, in Jesus' Name. Amen.

MEDITATE ON THESE PASSAGES

James 1:17 (GNB) *"Every good gift and every perfect present comes from heaven; it comes down from God, the Creator of the heavenly lights, who does not change or cause darkness by turning."*

Hebrews 9:14 (GNB) *"Since this is true, how much more is accomplished by the blood of Christ! Through the eternal Spirit, He offered Himself as a perfect sacrifice to God."*

Hebrews 12:23-4 (GNB) *"You have come to the joyful gathering of God's people whose names are written in heaven. You have come to God, who is the judge of all people, and to the spirits of good people made perfect. You have come to Jesus, who arranged the new covenant … His sprinkled blood promises much better things …"*

■ ■ ■   ■ ■◀◆▶■   ■   ■ ■ ■

"For in many things we offend all. If any man offend not in word, the same is a perfect man, and able also to bridle the whole body."
(**James 3:2 KJV**)

Yes, You Can Be A Perfect Man

◀ WEEK 43 ▶

God is really working on me, making me grow up and mature! He wants each of us to hear Him for ourselves! He wants us to obey what He speaks to us and not depend on what another human being may require of us.

Last month I phoned the prison where we minister to verify that it was open for the Ark's chapel service. The prison had been on 'lockdown' due to a big problem. I was told it was open now (that Friday) but to call Saturday morning to be sure no lockdown was in effect. I obeyed.

Only automated messages were available when I called on Saturday. I got no response to emails or phone messages left for the Chaplain. After five hours of automated messages stating: "...away from my desk, leave your phone number and I'll call back," I made our decision. I said to my husband and ministry partner: "No one is returning my calls. They must be back on lockdown. Something's going on. I don't want to make a two and a half- to three-hour drive and not be able to go in."

My husband, Garry, and I were both tired from very busy schedules. We chose not to go. Later, I learned that the prison had not been on lockdown. The chapel had been open to us.

The next month, it was the same scenario. However, this time, while studying and preparing my message, God Himself suddenly changed the message! The Holy Spirit spoke clearly: "The men need to be encouraged to praise Me! Someone needs to warn, urge and encourage them." God told me to ask the men, "What's your excuse? Where is your joy in the Lord?" Since we know the joy of our Lord is our strength, are we allowing Satan the thief to *"rob, steal and so destroy or devour us..."*? **(John 10:10 NIV)** I made a poor decision the previous month and lost my joy. God wanted the inmates to see that such things can happen---even to ministers.

The Scripture I was studying when God changed my message was **(Luke 14:15-24 GNB)**. We will look at specific parts here, but please read this in your Bible and the Good News Bible, too.

In this parable of the great feast, Jesus was sharing how a self-centered commitment can change things. When it was time for this feast, a servant was sent to tell the invited guests, *"Everything is ready. But, they all began, one after another, to make excuses."* **(Luke 14:18 GNB)** The guests had all accepted the invitation, but when the time came, they all began backing out, giving different excuses and rationalizations why they couldn't come now that the date had arrived. One just bought a field, one wanted to try out new oxen, one just got married, and so forth. Each apologized for the reason given that, at the last minute, he could not come. The angered master was furious and sent this same servant to the streets and alleys of the town and, finally, "...*out to the country roads and lanes to make people come in, so that my house will be full.*" **(Luke 14:23)**

When we accept an invitation, vow a vow, agree to do something, give our "yes", we are each responsible for fulfilling our "yes", our vow. Weddings are not normally last minute occasions. Usually, if we buy something, we research and try it out before purchasing. There are legalities to purchasing fields and land such as surveys, payments and signatures. These things take time. You know in advance and need to plan ahead to get them done. Sometimes we make a poor decision based on not getting the information we should have. The warning to me for that Saturday was biblical: I should do what I committed to do, regardless of what I think. This is how I honor God. Rather than apologizing, excusing or rationalizing to the prisoners, Garry and I asked forgiveness for our last-minute, self-centered change of plans the prior month. Jesus, Himself, set the example of finishing what He started. When we commit, He told us to follow His example and finish the work.

Now read **Thessalonians 2:15-17** in your version of the Bible. Here, I also used the Good News Bible: "*We must thank God at all times ...friends, you whom the Lord loves ...God chose you ...to be saved by the Spirit's power to make you His holy people by your faith in the truth. God called you to this through the good news we preached to you; He called you to possess your share of the glory of our Lord Jesus Christ. So then, our friends, stand firm and hold on to those truths which we taught you... May our Lord Jesus Christ Himself and God our Father, who loved us and in His grace gave us unfailing courage and a firm hope, encourage you, and strengthen you to always do and say what is good.*"

Changes are being made all over the world, not only in prisons and governments, but also in nature with extreme weather conditions! Inmates, friends and readers, forgive me. I make no apologies. That month we did not go to the prison, God strengthened me by allowing me to face the need to seek Him versus my own or another's reasoning! The next month, I did not wait for self-evaluation and then act on my own thinking, but rather, I listened to Father God, Jesus Christ and the Holy Spirit. Guess what? My joy returned along with my new understanding!

We must each hear God for ourselves. Know His voice and obey! If He told me to share these Scriptures at the prison, then He will get me inside, legally! If we drive all the way there and can't get in the chapel, He will make His reason perfectly clear. He knew me before I was a *"seed in my mother's womb"* (**Deuteronomy 30:19 GNB**) and He knows you, too. He knows everyone. He knows all there is to know!

Self, friends, everyone: Don't murmur and grumble about who didn't do what. Trust God! Hear His voice and obey quickly! Let there be no forty-year wandering to the Promised Land like the Israelites did in the desert. Remember, that was really only an eleven day trip! Holy Spirit, strengthen each of us to not make excuses or blame someone else. Accepting responsibility for what we say and do is part of God's plan and process of perfection.

PRAYER

Father, in light of Your Word and through Holy Spirit guidance, strengthen and encourage each of us to 'lean not to [our] own understanding' or dependency on people. Lead us not to offense, but to listen and know Your voice. You have given the ministry of reconciliation to each of us. Help us hear You clearly, share the good news and do what You require and ask us to do. Thank You for choosing us and encouraging and strengthening us, in Jesus' Name. Hallelujah! Amen.

MEDITATE ON THESE PASSAGES

Romans 12:2 (NIV) *"Do not conform any longer to the pattern of this world, but be transformed by the renewing of your mind. Then you will be able to test what God's will is – His good, pleasing and perfect will."*

James 1:22-25 (GNB) *"Do not deceive yourselves by just listening to His word... practice... look close into the perfect law that sets people free... you will be blessed."*

James 3:2 (NLT) *"Indeed, we all make many mistakes. For if we could control our tongues, we would be perfect and could also control ourselves in every other way."*

Luke 14:15-24 (GNB) *"When one of the guests sitting at the table heard this, he said to Jesus, "How happy are those who will sit down at the feast in the Kingdom of God!" When it was time for the feast, he sent his servant to tell his guests, 'Come, everything is ready!'*

But they all began, one after another, to make excuses. The first one told the servant, 'I have bought a field and must go and look at it; please accept my apologies.' Another one said, 'I have bought five pairs of oxen and am on my way to try them out; please accept my apologies.' Another one said, 'I have just gotten married, and for that reason I cannot come.' The servant went back and told all this to his master. The master was furious and said to his servant, 'Hurry out to the streets and alleys of the town, and bring back the poor, the crippled, the blind, and the lame.' Soon the servant said, 'Your order has been carried out, sir, but there is room for more.' So the master said to the servant, 'Go out to the country roads and lanes and make people come in, so that my house will be full. I tell you all that none of those who were invited will taste my dinner!'"

■ ■ ■   ■   ■◄◆►■   ■   ■ ■ ■

"...in order to present the church to Himself in all its beauty - pure and faultless, without spot or wrinkle or any other imperfection."
(Ephesians 5:27 GNB)

Christ Loved The Church and Gave His Life For It

◄ WEEK 44 ►

In **(Ephesians 5 GNB)** we are warned to *"be careful how we live..."* We are told not to live like *"ignorant people"* and to *"make good use of every opportunity... because these days are evil."* **(verses 6-8)** We are warned and told not to behave like fools, but to *"find out what the Lord wants you to do."* We were warned that too much wine (alcohol) *"... will only ruin you; instead be filled with the Spirit."* **(verses 16-18)** We are exhorted to *"speak to one another with the words of psalms, hymns, and sacred songs; sing hymns and psalms to the Lord with praise in our hearts."* **(verse 19)** We are to understand that both actions are necessary - encouragement to others and praises to God. Then, it is mandated in **verse 20**: *"In the name of our Lord Jesus Christ, always give thanks for everything to God the Father."* **(Ephesians 5:15-20 GNB)**

I hear too much murmuring, complaining, faultfinding and blaming of others, rather than self-examination and repentance. We are told to be like Him (**Ephesians 5:1b GNB**). We are not to be *"so zealous that we persecute the church..."* and if we continue reading we learn that *"...The knowledge of Christ Jesus as Lord..."* is much more valuable than appearing righteous or having reckless obedience to a particular belief or mindset. Paul reminds us there is *"no righteousness of our own, the kind... gained by obeying the Law..."* or our own works. *"Righteousness... is given through faith in Christ, the righteousness that comes from God and is based on faith."* All we need to know is *"...Christ, and to experience the power of His resurrection, to share in His sufferings and become like Him..."* (**Philippians 3:6-10 GNB**)

We are *"...urged ...to live a life that measures up to the standard God set when He called you."* That is perfect! He gives no preferential treatment. He called each of us to *"...be always humble, gentle, and patient... to show love by being tolerant with one another..."* doing our *"best to preserve the unity which the Spirit gives by means of the peace that binds us together. There is one body and one Spirit... one hope to which God has called..."* each of us. (**Ephesians 4:1-4 GNB**)

We are one church. *"There is one Lord, one faith, one baptism... one God and Father of all people, who is Lord of all, works through all, and is in all. Each one of us has received a special gift in proportion to what Christ has given... It was He who gave gifts to people; He appointed some to be apostles, others to be prophets... evangelists... pastors and teachers. He did this to prepare all God's people for the work of Christian service, in order to build up the body of Christ."* (**Ephesians 4:7-12 GNB**)

This then, is the Church---Christ's Church. We will be *"...mature people, reaching to the very height of Christ's full stature."* (**Ephesians 4:13 GNB**) That maturity is the perfection the Father wants each of us to reach.

PRAYER

Father, we want your will in our lives today. Help us to become mature people, to "put childish ways behind" us as in (1 Corinthians 13:11b NIV) *and to follow the leading of the Holy Spirit, in the Name of Jesus Christ. Amen.*

MEDITATE ON THESE PASSAGES

Philippians 1:9-10 (NIV) *"And this is my prayer: that your love may abound more and* *more in knowledge and depth of insight, so that you may be able to discern what is best and may be pure and blameless for the day of Christ..."*

Ephesians 5:25-27 (GNB) *"Christ loved the church and gave His life for it ...making it clean by washing it in water, in order to present the church to Himself in all its beauty – pure and faultless, without spot or wrinkle or any other imperfection."*

I John 4:18 (GNB) *"There is no fear in love; perfect love drives out all fear. So then, love has not been made perfect in anyone who is afraid, because fear has to do with punishment."*

I Corinthians 13:11 (NIV) *"When I was a child, I talked like a child, I thought like a child, I reasoned like a child. When I became a man, I put childish ways behind me."*

NOTES: _____

_____

_____

_____

_____

_____

_____

_____

_____

_____

_____

_____

_____

DIRECTION: _____

_____
_____
_____
_____
_____
_____
_____
_____
_____
_____

PROGRESS: _____

_____
_____
_____
_____
_____
_____
_____
_____
_____
_____

■■■   ■   ■◄◆►■   ■   ■■■

*"Therefore leaving the principles of the doctrine of Christ, let us go on unto perfection;
not laying again the foundation of repentance from dead works,
but of faith toward God... and this will we do, if God permit."*
(Hebrews 6:1, 3 Scofield)

Let Us Go On Unto Perfection

◄ *WEEK 45* ►

Let us come to God: spend time alone with Him daily; be devoted to Him, led by Him, filled with His Spirit, taught by Him and so be kept from sinning. Jesus never said or did anything but what His Father God spoke or saw Him do. **(John 5:19 GNB)** Jesus told us to follow His example. **(Matthew 16:24 AMP)**

"May the God of peace make you holy through and through. May you be kept in soul and mind and body in spotless integrity until the coming of our Lord Jesus Christ." **(I Thessalonians 5:23 Phillips)** Spotless integrity? That is perfection!

Reading and praying **(Revelation 3:1-3 GNB)**, we are reminded how Father God, Jesus Christ and the Holy Spirit *"know what you are doing..."* It says to *"wake up and strengthen what you have before it dies completely. For I find that what you have done is not yet perfect in the sight of God. Remember then, what you were taught and what you heard; obey it and turn from your sins..."*

Praise God! He never changes and His love is steadfast. His desire is to love us into being perfect children, according to **(Philippians 2:15 GNB)** *"But if we confess our sin to God, He will keep His promise and do what is right; He will forgive us our sins and purify us from all wrongdoing."* **(1 John 1:9 GNB)** That is His perfecting process. Daily we must spend time alone with God. *"This is how we can be sure that we are in union with God. If we say that we remain in union with God, we should live just as Jesus Christ."* **(I John 2:6 GNB)**

It is in obedience that we become sure that we know Him. *"If we obey His Word, we are the ones whose love for God has really been made perfect."* **(I John 2:5a GNB)** Again, Jesus said, *"I am the way and the truth and the life. No one comes to the Father except through me. If you really knew me you would know my Father as well. From now on, you do know Him and have seen Him... anyone who has seen me has seen the Father... I am in the Father and the Father is in me... the words I say to you are not just my own. Rather, it is the Father, living in me, who is doing His work."* **(John 14:6-10 NIV)**

The life of Jesus clearly and perfectly mirrors our heavenly Father and His work. We, too, must reflect the love made manifest in Jesus. Jesus told us to go, to give, to shine His love to the entire world!

PRAYER

Father, bring us closer to you; strengthen us to build rich friendships which are rooted and grounded in You! Teach us how to avoid selfishness and possessiveness, so we are free to be Your love for others, daily! I pray this in the Name of my Savior, Your Son, Jesus. Amen.

MEDITATE ON THESE PASSAGES

Matthew 6:48 (AMP) *"You, therefore, must be perfect [growing into complete maturity of Godliness in mind and character, having reached the proper height of virtue, integrity], as your heavenly Father is perfect."*

I John 4:17 (NKJV) *"Love has been perfected among us in this: that we may have boldness in the day of judgment; because as He is, so are we in this world."*

1 John 4:18 (NKJV) *"There is no fear in love; but perfect love casts out fear, because fear involves torment. But he who fears has not been made perfect in love."*

Psalms 19:13 (GNB) *"Keep me safe, also from willful sins; don't let them rule over me. Then I shall be perfect and free from the evil of sin."*

... ▪ ◄◆►▪ ▪ ...

*"But whoso keepeth His word, in him verily is the love of God perfected:
hereby know we that we are in Him."*
(1 John 2:5 Scofield)

Are We in Him?

◄ WEEK 46 ►

In Jesus, we are in the love of God! Love is the key that opens doors to encourage us *"that we may prove what is the good and acceptable, and perfect will of God."* **(Romans 12:2b Scofield)**

The first part of that verse warns us, *"be not conformed to this world: be ye transformed by the renewing of your mind..."* **(Romans 12:2a Scofield)**

Paul is not telling us to live in a state of super-spirituality, for that would be hypocrisy. Jesus loved the world of nature: working with His hands as a carpenter; playing with and loving little children; and doing ordinary things like cooking and eating fish. I do, too! How about you?

At times, my husband and I go away from work to see the beauty of nature in this world. God created all of nature: waterfalls, fall or spring foliage, snow, glaciers, palm trees, sandy beaches, and more. These refresh me! When I'm having a difficult day, Father God usually sends me a little child for activities like rocking a baby, 'high fives', playing games or sharing at children's church. He knows His joy will flood my soul and heal my spirit. Working with my hands: cooking, decorating, caring for houseplants, and other household cleaning also help restore my heart and soul!

Jesus set that example for us. But His greatest and highest service was to His Father. He often took time to be alone with His Father. We need to follow that example too! To be whole, we must spend time alone with Father God daily. Remember, we are *"to present our bodies as a living sacrifice, holy and acceptable unto God, which is... reasonable service."* **(Romans 12:1-3 Scofield)**

Time with Him strengthens and encourages us to work through difficult relationships and circumstances and enter into reconciliation. This frees us to love as Jesus, Father God and the Holy Spirit lead the way or make possible the way of healing and rescue. Alone with our Triune God, we can receive *"comfort in all our affliction, so that we may be able to comfort those who are in any affliction, with the comfort with which we ourselves are comforted by God."* **(II Corinthians 1:4 RSV)**

"Brethren, I do not consider that I have made it my own; but one thing I do. Forgetting what lies behind and straining forward to what lies ahead, I press on toward the goal for the prize of the upward call of Christ Jesus. May the God of peace Himself sanctify you wholly; and may your spirit and soul and body be kept sound and blameless at the coming of our Lord Jesus Christ." **(Philippians 3:13-14 RSV)**

And that, my dear friends, is perfect.

PRAYER

Father, may Thy will and Thy Kingdom come---as You deliver us from the evil one by the power of the Holy Spirit under the blood of Jesus. Amen.

MEDITATE ON THESE PASSAGES

Hebrews 10:19-22 (NIV) *"Therefore brethren, since we have confidence to enter the sanctuary by the blood of Jesus, by the new and living way which He opened for us through the curtain, that is, through His flesh...let us draw near..."*

Isaiah 59:20-21 (NIV) *"The Redeemer will come...to those...who repent of their sins, declares the Lord, as for me, this is My covenant with them... My Spirit, who is on you, and My words that I have put in your mouth will not depart from your mouth or from the mouths of your children...their descendants from this time on and forever..."*

Samuel 2:33 (KJV) *"God is my strength and power: and He maketh my way perfect."*

∎∎∎　∎　∎◀◆▶∎　∎　∎∎∎

*"Moses listened to his father-in-law and did everything he said. Moses chose capable men…
and made them leaders of the people, officials over thousands, hundreds, fifties and tens."*
(Exodus 18:24-25 GNB)

Release His Anointing

◀ WEEK 47 ▶

As I've said, the call on my life is to work with people, pre-teens through 40 years old. I train leadership. This takes time, prayer and study of the Word. Each person must know God in an intimate, personal and powerful way that follows the example of Jesus. There are basic life lessons to learn: being faithful, being on time and finishing what we start. Each leader must recognize his or her God-given gift! Each one must practice this gift within the body of Christ (the Church).

Each faithfully trained volunteer must learn to responsibly release his or her anointing (God's blessing or call on your life) to help others. Each one must be a team worker who can submit to the authority of leaders and elders (because this multiplies our anointing so it flows through us to others). Each leader must cooperate to help those needing to receive God's guidance and truth. As **(2 Corinthians 1:11 AMP)** says, *"While you also cooperate by your prayers for us (helping and laboring together with us), thus (the lips of) many persons (turned to God will eventually) give thanks on our behalf for the grace (the blessing of deliverance) granted us at the request of the many who have prayed."*

Moses' father-in-law saw the need to delegate responsibilities instead of trying to do everything himself. Training leadership means finding the right people. It means putting them in place and letting them do their work. Workaholics and codependents need to realize (as Moses did) when they are taking on too much responsibility. Training leaders means letting them learn from their mistakes. Each must be encouraged to find practical, spiritual solutions to daily problems. Each faithful, trained volunteer must dedicate himself or herself to prayer and study of the Word. When that happens, all leaders, pastors, staff, and volunteer leadership positions will carry a greater dimension of anointing to people in need.

As we allow ourselves to submit to our Lord and His guidelines for leadership more people will be helped. (Please read in your own Bible: **Romans 13:1-6, Colossians 3:22-25,** and **I Thessalonians 5:12.**) Others will see our life examples. Look at Paul struggling with his *"thorn in the flesh."* **(2 Corinthians 12:7 NIV)** Jesus spoke to him saying, *"My grace is sufficient for you, for my strength is made perfect in weakness..."* Paul gave a faith-filled response; he wrote, *"Therefore most gladly I will rather boast... in weaknesses, in insults, in hardships, in persecutions, in difficulties. For when I am weak, then I am strong."* **(2 Corinthians 12:9-10 NIV)** Why would Paul say that? When he admits his weakness, then he must turn to the source of his strength, Jesus. When we make decisions to run our own lives from our selfish needs or choices we lose the powerful strength of Jesus. Jesus had a plan for handling that and sent out teams of two or more. We too, can receive strength and pleasure, even in hardship, when we pair ourselves with Jesus and we can then also bear much more good fruit.

After a very busy day, cooperating with a team, many people will be helped and healed… focus now, on Jesus' and His action: *"Very early the next morning, long before daylight, Jesus got up and left the house. He went out of town to a lonely place, where He prayed. But, Simon and his companions went out searching for Him, and when they found Him, they said, 'Everyone is looking for you'... But Jesus answered, 'We must go on to the other villages around here. I have to preach for them also, because that is why I came.'* **(Mark 1:35-38 GNB)**

Leaders must develop and maintain the ability to work together! We must go out for alone time with God. We must listen, hear and obey. We must work in Godly teams. There is much work to do and laborers are few. Each one must hear God's call for his or her own self. Each of us must obey God rather than trying to always please people. Today is the day the Lord has made. I choose to rejoice and be glad in it! I hope you choose to rejoice and be glad too!

PRAYER

Father, I want more alone time with You! Please show and tell me what You want -- line upon line and precept upon precept -- as I continue to meditate on Your Word. I ask Jesus to shine powerfully and brightly into my daily fellowship and into the fellowship of my coworkers, those laboring in Your fields and the leaders to follow in bringing You glory. Amen

MEDITATE ON THESE PASSAGES

Mark 1:29-39 (CEV) *(Please read about Jesus going about His daily life using any translation you want.)* *"As soon as Jesus left the meeting place with James and John, they went home with Simon and Andrew. When they got there, Jesus was told that Simon's mother-in-law was sick in bed with fever. Jesus went to her. He took hold of her hand and helped her up. The fever left her, and she served them a meal. That evening after sunset, all who were sick or had demons in them were brought to Jesus. In fact, the whole town gathered around the door of the house. Jesus healed all kinds of terrible diseases and forced out a lot of demons. But the demons knew who he was, and he did not let them speak. Very early the next morning, Jesus got up and went to a place where he could be alone and pray. Simon and the others started looking for him. And when they found him, they said, "Everyone is looking for you!" Jesus replied, "We must go to the nearby towns, so that I can tell the good news to those people. This is why I have come." Then Jesus went to Jewish meeting places everywhere in Galilee, where he preached and forced out demons."*

Exodus 18:19-20 (NIV) *"Listen now to me and I will give you some advice, and may God be with you. You must be the people's representative before God and bring their disputes to Him. Teach them… laws … show them the way to live and the duties they are to perform."*

Psalms 4:8 (GNB) *"When I lie down, I go to sleep in peace; You alone O Lord, keep me perfectly safe."*

Exodus 18:21 (NIV) *"But select capable men from all people – men who fear God, trustworthy men who hate dishonest gain – and appoint them as officials over thousands, hundreds, fifties, and tens."*

James 3:2 (GNB) *"All of us often make mistakes. But if a person never makes a mistake in what he says, he is perfect and able to control his whole being."*

"All these promises are made to us, my dear friends.
So then, let us purify ourselves from everything that makes body or soul unclean,
and let us be completely holy by living in awe of God."
(II Corinthians 7:1 GNB)

Choose to Purify Ourselves and Be Completely Holy

◄ WEEK 48 ►

"Let us go forward! And this is what we will do ..." **(Hebrews 6:3 GNB)** God's will is to create "perfect children" **(Ephesians 4:13 AMP)** He wants His children to seek Christ's perfection and become mature (perfect) men or women who are serving Him. In this way we can complete our purpose. As described in **Romans 8:29**, God is working all things together to accomplish His purpose in us. *"In His life on earth, Jesus made His prayers and requests with loud cries, and tears to God... He was humble and devoted... Even though Jesus was God's Son, He learned through His sufferings to be obedient. When Jesus was made perfect, He became the source of eternal salvation for all those who obey Him, and God declared Him to be high priest..."* **(Hebrews 5:7-10 GNB)**

The writer(s) of Hebrews encourage us to follow the way of faith and to remain faithful to the end. This comes through spending daily time alone with Father God, Jesus and the Holy Spirit. This time of fellowship improves our personal relationship and refreshes us as we *"find grace to help us just when we need it."* **(Hebrews 4:16 GNB)** *"Let us go forward, then, to mature teaching and leave behind us the first teaching about baptisms and the laying on of hands; of the resurrection of the dead and the eternal judgment."* **(Hebrews 6:1-3a GNB)** Note, that the Scripture doesn't say to forget about the first teaching; it says to move on and learn more.

We are to become like Jesus and need to do the things He did. As we spend time alone with Him, we renew our minds continually. *"The Word of God is alive and active, sharper than any double-edged sword. It cuts all the way through, to where soul and spirit meet, to where joints and marrow come together..."* **(Hebrews 4:12 GNB)** In this alone time with Him we become more intimate and see His goodness, experience His love. The

Holy Spirit is training and leading us to find His loving Presence.

Remember, we are told to *"lean not to our own understanding but to trust Him..."* (**Proverbs 3:5 NIV**) Understanding may fail us, but trust will keep us close to Him. We will sense His peace. He alone can calm our fears and clear our minds. If we listen to Him and tune out worldly voices we will hear Him more clearly. We were designed and created to dwell with Him in peace every day. Come now, let us draw near to Father God and receive His peace. *"For God so loved the world that He gave His only begotten Son, that whosoever believeth in Him should not perish, but have everlasting life."* (**John 3:16 KJV**)

Finally, *"trust in the Lord with all your heart. Never rely on what you think you know. Remember the Lord in everything you do and He will show you the right way. Never let yourself think you are wiser than you are; simply obey the Lord and refuse to do wrong. If you do, it will be like good medicine, healing your wounds and easing your pains. Honor the Lord by making him an offering from the best ..."* (**Proverbs 3:5-9 GNB**)

PRAYER

Father, thank you for your process which is working in my life to bring me to maturity in Christ. Help me to focus on You during this season. I humbly submit myself to You, because I know you have a good plan in store for me and mine! I choose to rest and trust in You. Thank You for cleansing my heart, in Jesus' Name. Amen.

MEDITATE ON THESE PASSAGES

Proverbs 3:11-12 (GNB) *"My child when the Lord corrects you, pay close attention and take it as a warning – the Lord corrects those He loves, as parents correct a child of whom they are proud."*

Proverbs 3:13, 15 (GNB) *"Happy is anyone who becomes wise... who comes to have understanding... wisdom is more valuable than jewels; nothing you could want can compare with it."*

Acts 23:1 (GNB) *"Paul looked straight at the Council and said...'my conscience is perfectly clear about the way in which I have lived before God to this very day.'"*

NOTES: _____

_____

_____

_____

_____

_____

_____

_____

_____

_____

_____

_____

_____

_____

_____

_____

_____

_____

_____

_____

_____

_____

_____

BECOMING PERFECT

DIRECTION: _____

_____

_____

_____

_____

_____

_____

_____

_____

_____

_____

_____

PROGRESS: _____

_____

_____

_____

_____

_____

_____

_____

_____

_____

"Jesus said to him, "If you want to be perfect, go and sell all you have and give the money to the poor and you will have riches in heaven; then come and follow me."
(Matthew 19:21 GNB)

Think of Us as Christ's Servants

◄ WEEK 49 ►

The rich young ruler heard what Jesus said in the Scripture above *"...and went away sad because he was very rich."* **(Matthew 19:22-23 GNB)** Jesus responded, *"I assure you; it will be very hard for rich people to enter the Kingdom of Heaven. I repeat, it is much harder for a rich person to enter the Kingdom of God than for a camel to go through the eye of a needle."* Note, that Jesus did not say it was impossible or that rich people can't enter, but that it would be 'very hard' and 'much harder' for them to enter the Kingdom. Also, the entry gate to Jerusalem was built so that camels had to kneel to go through. This was for security and was thus called the 'needle's eye'.

Even the twelve disciples questioned Him, saying, *"Who, then, can be saved?"* **(Matthew 19:25-26 GNB)** Note, Jesus' answer: *"This is impossible for human beings, but for God, everything is possible."*

After the death of my first husband, Sam, the Father asked me (and taught me through the doing of it) to serve at His House (the Ark of Faith Foundation) without pay. He wanted me to humble myself and submit like His Son, Jesus, who came to serve, not to be served, as is written in **Matthew 20:27**. My thinking was to question how this would work – I had three teenagers! He reminded me, *"I take care of widows and orphans."* **(Psalms 68:5 GNB)** Oh! I see... Yes, Lord, I will trust You. You do not lie. You keep Your promises. The resulting truth: My family has never been without anything we needed. We didn't necessarily get all that we may have wanted, but for godly desires, sooner or later, we usually received the "want" or something even better.

All of these Scriptures test our true desire to serve Him, to share our own abundance and care for needs of others.

BECOMING PERFECT

How I praise and honor Father God, my older brother Jesus and the Holy Spirit! Truly nothing is impossible with God. He is still teaching me and perfecting me. The requirement to forgive seventy times seven in order for me to be forgiven is still challenging. Sometimes my flesh just doesn't want to respond. Is forgiveness 'much harder' to get through than the needle's eye?

Paul states, *"I write this to you, not because I want to make you feel ashamed, but to instruct you as my own dear children."* (**I Corinthians 4:14 GNB**) He continues, *"It is not right for you to be proud! You know the saying, 'a little bit of yeast makes the whole batch of dough rise?' ...You must remove the old yeast of sin so that you will be entirely pure."* (**I Corinthians 5:6-7 GNB**) Readers, entirely pure equals perfect.

Sin is sin. Loving money more than God, greed or unforgiveness all are sins. The Father sent Jesus so that we might be set free and forgiven. Jesus is our 'show and tell' example from Father God. The restoration of the Holy Spirit to each of us comes through Jesus Christ, our faithful leader, guide, teacher, intercessor, and friend. Praise Father God for sending Jesus! I end today's lesson with this assurance: *"But, he who joins himself to the Lord becomes spiritually one with Him."* (**I Corinthians 6:17 GNB**)

PRAYER

Father God, thank You for leading and guiding me to victory in Christ Jesus. I choose to rely constantly on You. Send the Holy Spirit to help me as You give me opportunities today to share Your joy and love with the people around me in Jesus' Name. Amen.

MEDITATE ON THESE PASSAGES

I Corinthians 4:1 (AMP) *"So then, let us [apostles] be looked upon as ministering servants of Christ, and stewards (trustees) of the mysteries (secret purposes) of God."*

I Corinthians 4: 20-21 (GNB) *"...For the Kingdom of God is not a matter of words but of power. Which do you prefer? Shall I come to you with a whip, or in a spirit of love and gentleness?"*

I Corinthians 6:11 (GNB) *"Some of you were like that. But you have been purified from sin; you have been dedicated to God; you have been put right with God by the Lord Jesus*

Christ and by The Spirit of our God!"

I Corinthians 6:19-20 (GNB) *"Don't you know your body is the temple of the Holy Spirit, who lives in you and who was given to you by God; He bought you for a price, so use your bodies for God's glory."*

■■■ ■ ■◀◆▶■ ■ ■■■

"We are glad when we are weak but you are strong.
And so we also pray that you will become perfect."
(II Corinthians 13:9 GNB)

We Pray You Will Become Perfect

◀ WEEK 50 ▶

"Put yourself to the test and judge yourself, to find out whether you are living in faith. Surely you know that Christ is in you? Unless you have completely failed, I trust you will know that we are not failures... For we cannot do a thing against the truth, but only for it. We are glad when we are weak but you are strong. And so we also pray that you will become perfect. That is why I write this while I am away from you; it is so that when I arrive I will not have to deal harshly with you in using the authority the Lord has given me – the authority to build you up, not to tear you down. And now, my friends... strive for perfection... live in peace. And the God of love and peace will be with you... the grace of the Lord Jesus Christ, the love of God, and the fellowship of the Holy Spirit be with you all." **(II Corinthians 13:5-13 GNB)**

To follow the Scripture, each of us must pray to be perfect. We must strive and work hard to be perfect. My part (as wife, mother, grandmother, Direct of Operations at the Ark of Faith Foundation, a chaplain in prison and hospital ministry...) is to pray **(II Corinthians 1:11 AMP)** that each of us *"will become perfect... as we cooperate by your prayers for us helping and laboring together with us, thus the lips of many persons turned toward God will eventually give thanks on our behalf for the grace (the blessing of deliverance) granted us at the request of the many."* The King James version says it, *"...you also, helping together in prayer for us, that thanks may be given by many persons on our behalf* *for the gift granted to us through many."*

This gift is not by fleshly wisdom but rather, by the abundant grace of God through Jesus Christ and the Holy Spirit's leading. More and more, I am using **Proverbs 22:6** as a teaching. It says: *"Train up a child in the way he should go, and when he is old he will not depart from it."* As I studied, I saw a footnote that led me to also read **(Ephesians 6:4 AMP)**: *"Fathers, do not irritate and provoke your children to anger, do not exasperate them to resentment, but rear them [tenderly] in training and discipline and the counsel and admonition of the Lord."*

Love wins! If we love God, we obey Him. *"If you don't punish them, you don't love them. If you love them; you will correct them."* **(Proverbs 22:6 NKJV)** *"Discipline your children while they are young enough to learn. If you don't, you are helping them destroy themselves."* **(Proverbs 19:18 GNB)**

Today, God is reminding me to continue praying for my adult children, grandchildren and my young great grandchildren to become perfect! Still, each child must come to God alone, by his or her unique and individual 'gifting', by giving his or her 'best.' Each child must be trained and corrected by parents. But at adulthood (18 years old in USA), each person must accept that role and exercise his or her own choices and be accountable for using his or her own gifts (abilities).

"When I was a child, my speech, feelings, and thinking were all those of a child …" That was (and still is) true of me, at times. The Word goes on: *"…now that I am an adult, I have no more use for childish ways."* **(1 Corinthians 13:11 GNB)** Yes, my parents trained me; they did not enable me or let me become co-dependent on them. Thank you, Jesus. You are the Truth (the Way) and You brought me the Helper through my parents. But they also had to let go of their desires and control to allow Father God do the actual work. We can pray, but we cannot actually make people change.

I must spend time alone with Father God, Jesus and the Holy Spirit. Each of us must come to God alone. *"Love never gives up; and its faith, hope, and patience never fail. Love is eternal. There are inspired messages, but they are temporary; there are gifts of speaking in strange tongues, but they will cease; there is knowledge, but it will pass. For our gifts of knowledge and of inspired messages are only partial; but when what is perfect comes, then what is partial will disappear."* **(I Corinthians 13:4-10 GNB)**

Finally, *"Love bears up under anything and everything that comes, is ever ready to believe the best of every person; its hopes are fadeless under all circumstances, and it endures everything [without weakening]."* **(1 Corinthians 13:7 AMP)** Father God, Jesus Christ and the Holy Spirit are eager and waiting to help each of us grow into mature people who can fulfill our God-given purposes.

PRAYER

Father, thank You for the enduring faith and hope and eagerness of the Holy Spirit to strengthen and help each of us grow up and put away childish behavior. Deliver each of us from making decisions out of our emotions. Thank You, Jesus, for shedding Your blood for our forgiveness and sending the Holy Spirit to guide us on our journey to be like You. Amen.

MEDITATE ON THESE PASSAGES

Proverbs 4:1-5 (GNB) *"My children listen to what your father teaches you. Pay attention... remember it all. When I was only a little boy... my father would teach me and say, 'Remember what I say... do as I tell you and you will live.'"*

Proverbs 4:10-24 (GNB) *"Listen to me my child, take seriously what I am telling you... I have taught you wisdom and the right way to live... Be careful how you think; your life is shaped by your thoughts... have nothing to do with lies and misleading words.*

Roman 8:28 (AMP) *"We are assured and know that [God being a partner in their labor] all things work together and are [fitting into a plan] for good to and for those who love God and are called according to [His] design and purpose.*

Luke 8:15 (NIV) *"Therefore consider carefully how you listen. Whoever has will be given more; whoever does not have, even what he thinks he has will be taken away from him."*

■■■ ■ ▄◀◆▶▄ ■ ■■■

The Law of Moses appoints men who are imperfect to be high priests;
but God's promise made with the vow which cancels later than the Law appoints the Son,
who has been made perfect forever."
(Hebrews 7:28 GNB)

The Son Who Has Been Made Perfect Forever

◀ *WEEK 51* ▶

"*The whole point of what we are saying is that we have such a High Priest, who sits at the right of the throne of the Divine Majesty in heaven. He serves as high priest in the Most Holy Place; that is, in the real tent which was put up by the Lord, not by human hands.*" This eighth chapter of Hebrews (please do read it in your Bible) goes on to say, "*...Jesus has been given priestly work which is superior to theirs ...and is based on promises of better things ...In the days to come, says the Lord: I will put my laws in their minds and write them on their hearts. I will be their God, and they will be my people.*"
(Hebrews 8:1-10 GNB)

"*...Offerings and animal sacrifices presented to God cannot make the worshiper's heart perfect... food, drink and various purification ceremonies... are all outward rules... until the time when God will establish a new order...*" Through His blood, Christ accomplished much more than we understand. Please continue with these verses, "*...Through the eternal Spirit He offered Himself a perfect sacrifice to God: His blood will purify our consciences from useless rituals, so that we may serve the living God.*"
(Hebrews 9:10-14 GNB)

Making time to focus on Jesus, Father God and the Holy Spirit should be our highest priority and deepest joy! The longer we push Jesus into the background of our busy lives the harder it is to find His peace, love and moment-by-moment closeness and fellowship! The world, with its nonstop demands, can be put on hold. Rationalizing that one day soon we'll find time to focus on Him often allows the things of this world to control our lives.

PRAYER

Holy Spirit, strengthen and help us choose the better way. I love to hear the words of the praise song by Rich Mullins,
"Step by step You'll lead me / And I will follow you all of my days..."

Let each of us choose the better thing so we can bless others through You, Father God! I ask this in Jesus' Name, Amen.

MEDITATE ON THESE PASSAGES

Hebrews 9:24 (GNB) *"For Christ did not go into a Holy Place made by human hands, which is a copy of the real one. He went into heaven itself, where He now appears on our behalf in the presence of God."*

Hebrews 10:22 (GNB) *"So let us come near to God with a sincere heart and a sure faith, with hearts that have been purified from a guilty conscience and bodies washed with clean water."*

I Corinthians 13:8-11 (Weymouth) *"Love never fails. But if there are prophecies, they will be done away with; if there are languages, they will cease; if there is knowledge, it will be brought to an end. For our knowledge is imperfect, and so is our prophesying; but when the perfect state of things is come, all that is imperfect will be brought to an end."*

I Corinthians 13:12b-13 (Weymouth) *"...for the present, the knowledge I gain is imperfect; but then I shall know fully, even as I am fully known. So there remain FAITH, HOPE, LOVE---these three; and of these, the greatest is LOVE."*

II Corinthians 5:17 (NIV) *"Therefore if anyone is in Christ, he is a new creation, the old has gone, the new has come."*

... . ◄◆► . ...

"Therefore you shall be perfect, just as your Father in heaven is perfect."
(Matthew 5:48 GNB)

Just as Your Father in Heaven is Perfect

◄ WEEK 52 ►

We were created in whose image? God's! God is love! He is not just a loving and forgiving God, but He is love! He created us to be love.

In her book *Switch on Your Brain*, Caroline Leaf states, "You are made from God's perfectness, but it is up to you to create your expertise in life. God gives us the blueprint, but we need to choose to make it happen." How I wish everyone would get her book and read it; absorb it! Thank you, Father God, for this teaching – how needed it is now!

A dear friend of mine frequently says that when the student is ready the teacher will appear. I am ready, are you? My husband, Garry also suggested that I re-read **Ecclesiastes 3:1** which I read in the **Good News Bible**. It says, *"Everything that happens in this world happens at the time God chooses..."* I hope you will read **Ecclesiastes 3** in your own Bible, too!

It seems like wherever I am these days, I see the **(Matthew 5:48 GNB)** Scripture: *"Be perfect, just as your Father in heaven is perfect."* We can be perfect. We can, if we continue to seek Him, learn about Him, *"...press on toward the mark [goals] for which God has called me [each of us] heavenward in Christ Jesus ..."* **(Philippians 3:14 AMP)** Each of us must renew our minds daily as **(Romans 12:2 GNB)** advises, *"Do not conform yourselves to the standards of this world, but let God transform you inwardly by a complete change of your mind. Then you will be able to know the will of God---what is good and is pleasing to Him and is perfect."* I'd been praying, hoping, working and desiring daily renewal. What I appreciated about Caroline Leaf's book was that it tells me how.

As we open the Ark of Faith each day, we read what we call our "Proverbs of the Day". God has been also leading me to re-read my own book Alone with God at Christmas. I look back and see the word perfect in it as well. The world kept telling me that, "No one but Jesus is perfect." Yet, thank you, Holy Spirit, for never giving up on me! I'm not a quitter but, how much I needed this teaching at this time in my life. My mind is still being transformed. Oh God, thank You for Caroline Leaf and her book that assures we can physically change our minds..

"O Lord, You are my God. I will exalt You! I will praise Your name! For You have done wonderful things! Your counsels of old are faithfulness and truth!" (**Isaiah 25:1 GNB**) God is the great Scientist, as well as the great Physician! Recently, while I was praying for my husband while he worked on electrical things in a rental property, I paused. I thought: *You, Father, are the great Electrician just as You are the great Physician. You are my all in all...*

Each of us was created in His image. Each child is a gift from God and each one of us is gifted and unique. *"At one time you were far away from God and were His enemies because of the evil things you did and thought. But now, by means of the physical death of His Son, God has made you His friends in order to bring you, holy, pure and faultless into His presence."* (**Colossians 1:21 GNB**) Caroline Leaf's book reminds us of toxic thinking and our choice to speak only good and tell about God's work. *"We must not allow ourselves to be shaken from the hope gained when you heard the gospel..."* (**Colossians 1:23 GNB**)

Thank you, Father, for our ministry at the Ark of Faith and all who help serve and sustain it. *"...for the sake of His body, which is the Church, of which I became a minister according to the stewardship from God which was given to me for you, to fulfill the word of God... revealed to His saints... to make known... which is Christ in you, the hope of glory. Him we preach, warning every man and teaching every man in all wisdom, that we may present every man perfect in Christ Jesus."* (**Colossians 1:24b-28 NKJV**) *"As you therefore have received Christ Jesus the Lord, so walk in Him, rooted and built up in Him and established in the faith, as you have been taught, abounding in it with thanksgiving."* (**Colossians 2:6-7 NKJV**)

Thank you, God, for this privilege and opportunity to speak wholesome words, Your words; to create beauty, excellence and excitement; to be co-workers with God in today's world. *"Without You we can do nothing."* (**John 15:5 NKJV**) Since, as is written in **Genesis 17:1-2**, you have asked us to walk with You---blameless and perfect. Let us continue praying to be perfected by the Perfector.

PRAYER

Father, I want my days to be ordered by you. I want to see the turning points in my life. I need the Holy Spirit to strengthen and empower me to fulfill Your call on my life. I need Your grace and mercy. I love and bless You in Jesus' Name and by the power of Your Holy Spirit. Amen.

MEDITATE ON THESE PASSAGES

II Timothy 4:7 (KJV) *"I have fought a good fight, I have finished my course, I have kept the faith."*

John 15: 1-9 (GNB) *"I am the real vine, and my Father is the gardener. He breaks off every branch in me that does not bear fruit… remain in me and I will remain in you… you cannot bear fruit unless you remain in me… Those who remain in me, and I in them, will bear much fruit… My Father's glory is shown by your bearing much fruit… remain in my love."*

John 14:6 (GNB) *"Jesus answered him, "I am the way, the truth, and the life; no man goes to the Father except by me."*

John 16: 7 (Bible in Basic English/BBE) *"But what I am saying is true: my going is for your good: for if I do not go away, the Helper will not come to you; but if I go, I will send Him to you."*

NOTES: _____

_____

_____

_____

_____

_____

_____

_____

_____

NOTES:

DIRECTION: _____

_____
_____
_____
_____
_____
_____
_____
_____
_____
_____
_____

PROGRESS: _____

_____
_____
_____
_____
_____
_____
_____
_____
_____
_____
_____

Over Abundance
7 Additional Lessons from The Father

■ ■ ■   ■   ■◄◆►■   ■   ■ ■ ■

"For the eyes of the Lord run to and fro throughout the whole earth, to show Himself strong
in the behalf of them whose heart is perfect toward Him."
(II Chronicles 16:9 KJV)

Do We Have a Perfect Heart Toward Him?

◄ *Number 1* ►

I read many versions of the Bible in my search for deeper understanding. Read **II Chronicles 16:9** in your own Bible. Then read what I see in these versions (emphases mine):
- **New American Standard Bible**: *"…He may strongly support those whose **heart is completely His**…"*
- **New International Version**: *"…to strengthen those whose **hearts are fully committed** to Him…"*
- **Amplified Bible**: *"…those whose **hearts are blameless** toward Him…"*
- **New American Standard 1977**: *"…those who are devoted to Him **wholeheartedly**…"*

I thank God for this continuing study of perfecting, for His divine help, strength, support, and favor to help us become overcomers! This study continues to create in me a great desire to rise up and take responsibility to act on His Word! He continues to use my weaknesses and mistakes to His good purposes. When Father God sees that I do not want to compromise but am completely surrendered to Him, He becomes my Perfector. Do you find this is true for you?

BECOMING PERFECT

To fulfill our purpose it is necessary to have a daily surrendering of our wills and daily renewing of our minds to His Word! Yes, as **Romans 8:28** explains, God uses good and bad... when we love Him and heed His call to mature us for our individually created purpose! All of us are created in His image---the image of Love, created to Love.

Love can be given in many ways. You can: help change an elderly woman's flat tire, give a hug, a smile, a warm coat, a good meal or just a gentle word. The old saying that "it takes a village to raise a child" is so true. Love is a verb, a requirement to act; it is doing something. We are better when we are raised in a loving community. But, we don't always feel like being loving. What can we do when we are not always willing to act?

We must surrender our will to His. His Words in (**Luke 9:23 KJV**) are "...*if any man will come after me, let him deny himself, and take up his cross daily and follow me.*" Of course, we do not die on a wooden cross. Jesus denied himself in order to redeem us. Our 'cross' (or struggle; sometimes a tortured struggle) is to obey Him and do whatever He tells us to do. I'm finding that if I hear from God and do it immediately the results are miraculous! I also find that it is not always easy. I must 'die to (give up) my fleshly desires. I may not want to do it (that's the complete surrender---doing it when you don't feel like it). Still, I must do it as if I was doing it directly unto Jesus. Doing that requires facing my fears with His Holy Spirit power as referred to in **Philippians 4:13**. Using that faith, the victory comes through Him and in Him.

How do we "...*run with patience the race that is set before us, looking unto Jesus, the author and finisher of our faith; who for the joy that was set before Him, endured the cross, despising the shame, and is set down at the right hand of the throne of God...*" (**Hebrews 12:1-3 KJV**)

At the Ark of Faith, we find the "Joy of the Lord" is our strength and shield. I recommend singing that old, children's praise song when tempted to give in to fleshly tendencies. Our daily journey is in Him and with Him! We do not go out alone -- not to missions, not to preach, not to volunteer or serve, or even to church -- without the Holy Spirit, our Helper. He chose us to share the Good News. So, as even more praise songs and hymns say, we must "turn our eyes upon Jesus" and "step by step..." follow Him all the days of our lives. I find myself singing these old songs often. For me, faith also grows by hearing and singing hymns of praise. Let joy arise!

PRAYER

Father, you called each of us to go! As Proverbs 7 instructs, help us to recognize Your call and obey. Holy Spirit, help us not only to hear, but also to go with joy when we go out in Jesus' Name. Amen.

MEDITATE ON THESE PASSAGES

I Peter 2:9 (KJV) *"But ye are a chosen generation, a royal priesthood, an holy nation, a peculiar people; That ye should show forth the praises of Him who hath called you out of darkness into His marvelous light."*

John 10:3b-4 (GNB) *"...as He calls His own sheep by name and leads them out. When he has brought them out, he goes ahead of them, and the sheep follow him, because they know His voice."*

Proverbs 7:1-2 (GNB) *"My child, remember what I say and never forget what I tell you to do... and you will live. Be as careful to follow my teaching as you are to protect your eyes."*

■ ■ ■ ■ ◄◆► ■ ■ ■ ■

"Love is eternal ... for our gifts of knowledge and of inspired messages are only partial; but when what is perfect comes, what is partial will disappear."
(I Corinthians 13:9-10 GNB)

Let Every Temptation Add to Perfection

◄ *Number 2* ►

Practice to be perfect. Practice (whether piano, voice, football, typing, carpentry, public speaking, parenting, or using the character that Christ would have each of us develop) is a daily exercise.

Though He was perfect, we read that Jesus learned through His sufferings to be obedient and *"grew in wisdom and favor with God… When He was made perfect, He became the source of eternal salvation for all those who obey him…"* (**Hebrews 5:8-9 GNB**) We can be made perfect, too. In the midst of life, among men and things, troubles and difficulties, obstacles and overcoming, we learn to love!

We are told to watch and pray. That's not always easy. Skills and talents take practice. Talent often develops in times of solitude. There must be time set apart to develop our individual gifts. A specific time is necessary for each of us to see the unseen in prayer, faith, meditation, and fellowship with Father God, Jesus Christ and the Holy Spirit. Brother Lawrence, a 17th century Carmelite monk whose writings have been compiled and published, calls it *The Practice of the Presence of God*. (The book is available online and in bookstores. There are free versions.)

There must be time alone with God! Only as we fulfill the Word in the right conditions can we produce pure love. Look at (**I John 4:19 GNB**) *"We love because God first loved us."* We are not to isolate ourselves, but instead, to make a time for practice and solitude. That brings balance to our spirits and our lives. We will be changed into His image in this way---by repetitively practicing being like Him.

Love begets love. Paul says *"Love never fails."* (**Romans 8:39 ESV**) John tells us to *"… love one another, because love comes from God. Whoever loves is a child of God and knows God… if we love one another, God lives in union with us, and His love is made perfect in us…"*

We must practice and share God's love with others. Practice is an action. We get better and improve as we live in union with God and do what He commands. It takes both courage and practice to love. *"…There is no fear in love; perfect love drives out all fear…"* If unloved as a child or forsaken in adulthood, brokenness can short-circuit someone. *"…So then, love has not been made perfect in anyone who is afraid… Love is made perfect in us in order that we may have courage…"* (**I John 4:11-18 GNB**)

Judgment Day will come. However, moment by moment and day by day *"we win the victory over the world by means of our faith."* (**I John 5:4 GNB**) Both faith and love are action words. Action means doing, like practice---and with the Holy Spirit, practice does 'make perfect.'

If God made Jesus *"perfect through suffering"* (**Hebrews 2:10 GNB**), we, too, can expect some issues in our daily lives. Jesus never quit! Neither can we. To accomplish more we must put our mistakes, stumbles and failures under the blood of Jesus. He was and is our *"perfect sacrifice to God..."* and we do not have to die on the cross because He paid for our sins in full *"...so we may serve the living God."* **(Hebrews 9:14 GNB)** Our sins are washed away. We are forgiven by His blood. We are free to practice loving one another.

PRAYER

Dear Father, today like Paul did, "I pray that your love will keep on growing more and more, together with true knowledge and perfect judgment, so that you will be able to choose what is best." (Philippians. 1:9 GNB) Jesus, You are the Word. Fulfill this Scripture in me, my family, friends and readers so we may serve in the Name of the Living God. Amen.

MEDITATE ON THESE PASSAGES

Hebrews 6:1, 3 (NKJV) *"Therefore leaving the discussions of the elementary principles of Christ, let us go on unto perfection, not laying again the foundation of repentance from dead works ... and this will we do ...."*

Isaiah 26:3 (GNB) *"You, Lord, give perfect peace to those who keep their purpose firm and put their trust in You."*

I John 2:5 (GNB) *"But if we obey His work, we are the ones whose love for God has really been made perfect..."*

Hebrews 5:8-9 (GNB) *"But even though he was God's Son, he learned through his sufferings to be obedient. When he was made perfect, he became the source of eternal salvation for all those who obey him."*

Hebrews 6:1 (GNB) *"Let us go forward, then, to mature teaching and leave behind us the first lessons of the Christian message."*

■■■　　■　■◄◆►■　■　　■■■

"Put on therefore, as the elect of God, holy and beloved… mercies, kindness, humbleness of mind, meekness, longsuffering; forbearing one another and forgiving one another, if any men have a quarrel against any… forgive as Christ… and above all these things put on charity which is the bond of perfectness, and let the peace of God rule in your hearts…"
(I Colossians 3:12-15 KJV)

Put on the Bond of Perfectness

◄ *Number 3* ►

At any given moment, I may not be tender and kind toward those who do not love or please me. A melting process is needed inside my heart, as is daily 'dying to flesh' (giving up selfishness).

I had to learn not to pray for patience (because when I pray that way, patience develops through troubles, persecutions and other difficulties, as the Bible tells me in **Romans 5:3-4**. I don't want more of that than necessary. So, I now ask for the Holy Spirit to give me a gift of tenderness, kindness and generosity, or grace straight out of Father God's Spirit. *"The wisdom that is from above is first pure, then peaceable, gentle and easy to be entreated, full of mercy and good fruits without partiality and without hypocrisy."* **(James 3:17 KJV)**

(Revelations 3:2 GNB) says, *"…wake up, and strengthen what you still have before it dies completely; for I find that what you have done is not yet perfect in the sight of God."* God knows everything, sees everything; is the same yesterday, today and forever. Father God wants us to wake up and stop making excuses to avoid serving Him. Serving Him is our choice!

We are told to pray without ceasing and pray to be made perfect. Timothy urges *"…that petitions, prayers, requests and thanksgiving be offered to God for all people; for kings and all others who are in authority, that we may live a quiet and peaceful life with all reverence toward God and with proper conduct. This is good and pleases God our Savior who wants everyone to be saved and come to know the truth."* **(I Timothy 2:1-3 GNB)** This is His perfect will for each of us and explains His required daily service.

We are also told that *"those helpers who do their work well win for themselves a good standing and are able to speak boldly about their faith in Christ Jesus... This is how we should conduct ourselves in God's household ..."* **(I Timothy 3:12-15 GNB)**

"Everything God has created is good; nothing is to be rejected, but everything is to be received with a prayer of thanks, because the word of God and prayer make it acceptable to God..." This is part of the perfection process. *"...Until Jesus comes ..."* we are told *"to give our time and effort to the public reading of the Scriptures and to preaching and teaching ... not to neglect the spiritual gift that is in you ..."* **(I Timothy 4:4-14 GNB))**

Know that *"... the path of the [uncompromisingly] just and righteous is like the light of dawn that shines more and more (brighter and clearer) [until it reaches its full strength and glory in] the perfect day..."* **(Proverbs 4:18 AMP)**

If you bind yourself to this Godly goal of perfection, He will make you what you both desire.

PRAYER

Father, open my heart and mind to You so I can receive every blessing You have for me. Continue providing me with grace and mercy and everlasting favor throughout my troubles and struggles as I practice what You want me to be so I can mature! God, I need Your favor and man's favor to succeed in my life every day. In Jesus' holy Name I pray, Amen.

MEDITATE ON THESE PASSAGES

Proverbs 10:10 (AMP) *"He who winks with the eye [craftily and with malice] causes sorrow; the foolish of lips will fall headlong but he who boldly reproves makes peace."*

Philippians 2:15 (AMP) *"That you may show yourselves to be blameless and guileless, innocent and uncontaminated, children of God without blemish (faultless, unrebukeable) in the midst of a crooked and wicked generation [spiritually perverted and perverse], among whom you are seen as bright lights ... in the [dark] world."*

Romans 12:2 (AMP) *"And do not be conformed to this world... but be transformed by the renewing of your mind... so that you may prove... what is the good and acceptable and perfect will of God [in His sight for you]..."*

"And so we shall all come together to the oneness in our faith and in our knowledge of the Son of God; we shall become mature people, reaching to the very height of Christ's full stature."
(Ephesians 4:13 GNB)

That We May Grow Into the Fullness of Christ

◄ *Number 4* ►

Lord Jesus, You have made a way for the deliverance of all men from sin. In **Acts 8** we see that a man named Simon approached Peter and John wanting to buy the power he had witnessed when the Holy Spirit came down on the people of Samaria. *"He said, 'Give this power to me so that anyone I place my hands on will receive the Holy Spirit...' Peter answered him, 'May you and your money go to hell, for thinking that you can buy God's gift with money! You have no part or share in our work, because your heart is not right in God's sight. Repent, then of this evil plan of yours and pray to the Lord that He will forgive you for thinking such a thing as this. For I see that you are full of bitter envy and are a prisoner of sin."* **(Acts 8:19-23 GNB)**

One night, my husband, Garry, and I were doing our regular prison ministry. We brought the Good News to CCA Davis Correctional Center in Holdenville, Oklahoma. God had me share **(I John 4:7-21 GNB)** with the inmates. The word perfect was used four times. Read it, please, and know that, if we live in union with God: *"...His love is made perfect in us...God is love... those who live in union with God and God lives in union with them. Love is made perfect in us in order that we may have courage...There is no fear in love; perfect love drives out all fear. So then, love has not been made perfect in anyone who is afraid..."* **(I John 4:12-18 GNB)**.

Having read that Scripture, I was led to ask all those present to commit to three things in order to leave their pasts and shame behind them! I asked them: "Will you agree tonight to:
  1) Make a decision to perfect the love of God in your life;
  2) Constantly confess that you are the love of God and live the Word which says 'strive to be perfect'; and
  3) Continually and diligently practice the love of God by acting on His Word?"

Why am I bringing this word to each of you today? Because, as I followed my scheduled lectionary Scripture reading, I saw that something worse existed than being incarcerated within a state prison. I realized that, if we are full of envy, bitterness and hate, and if we murmur and grumble, then each one of us is *"...a prisoner of sin."* (**Acts 8:23 GNB**)

God is love. Created in His image, we are love. Father God made a way for our deliverance from sin by the death of Christ. It is our choice to confess and repent and daily renew our minds to the mind of Christ Who knew no sin. It is time to rejoice in this marvelous excellence of Christ's redemption of us. Let our goals be to first satisfy Father God in this love relationship that was prepared for us through Jesus, His Son.

PRAYER

Father, thank You for this new day and for choosing to use me for Your purpose. I want to accomplish the dreams and visions You purposed for me. I set my love on You today knowing You have something new in store for me. The best is yet to come from the Holy Spirit in Jesus' Name. Amen.

MEDITATE ON THESE PASSAGES

Romans 12:2 (NKJV) *"And do not be conformed to this world, but be transformed by the renewing of your mind so that you may prove what the will of God is; that which is good and acceptable and perfect."*

Romans 12:2 (NLT) *"Don't copy the behavior and customs of this world but let God transform you into a new person by changing the way you think. Then you will learn to know God's will for you, which is good and pleasing and perfect."*

II Timothy 2:15 (NASB) *"Be diligent to present yourself approved to God as a workman who does not need to be ashamed, accurately handling the word of truth."*

I John 4:11-12 (NIV) *"Dear friends, since God so loved us, we also ought to love one another. No one has ever seen God; but if we love one another, God lives in us and His love is made complete in us."*

Psalms 138:8 (AMP) *"The Lord will perfect that which concerns me; Your mercy and loving kindness, O Lord, endure forever; forsake not the works of Your own hands."*

■■■   ■ ■◄◆►■ ■   ■■■

"Having, therefore, these promises, dearly beloved, let us cleanse ourselves of all filthiness of the flesh and spirit; perfecting holiness in the fear of God."
(II Corinthians 7:1 KJV)

Perfecting Holiness in the Fear of God

◄ *Number 5* ►

"If we walk in the light, as He is the light, we have fellowship one with another, and the blood of Jesus Christ his Son cleanseth us from all sin." **(I John 1:7 KJV)**

How filthy have my hands and thoughts been, Lord? Holy Spirit, reveal it and lead me to You for a 'Spiritual scrubbing', as Catherine Marshall wrote in her book *My Personal Prayer Diary*. We have the mind of Christ. In this world *"a natural man does not accept the things of the Spirit of God, for they are foolishness to him; and he cannot understand them, because they are spiritually appraised... For who has known the mind of the Lord, that he will instruct Him? But we have the mind of Christ."* **(I Corinthians 2:14-16 NIV)** Father God wants each of us to have Christ's very own discernment (insight, understanding). As we yield to the Holy Spirit and the actual person of Jesus Christ the Redeemer, we can restructure our attitudes and perceptions.

Is anyone, besides me, facing difficulties, problems and temptations? We must overcome them! To the overcomer goes the victory. (Do read the entire book of Revelation in your own Bible. I am still learning to go there and not avoid it!) How do we overcome? *"We must renew our minds daily to the Word."* **(Romans 12:2 NLT)** We need the help of the Holy Spirit to *"... meditate on Your precepts and regard Your ways."* **(Psalms 119:15 NASB)** These Scriptures do not tell us to pray that God will renew our minds but that we must follow the Holy Spirit's initiatives.

If we are indeed called to be servants of God, **(Psalms 119:23 NASB)** reminds us, *"... Your servant meditates on Your statutes..."* and in the New Testament, *"Therefore if you have been raised up with Christ, keep seeking the things above... Set your mind on the things above and not on the things that are on earth. For you have died and your life is* *hidden with Christ in God.*" **(Colossians 3:1-3 NASB)**

Daily events require a response from us. Our response leads to an outcome---whether good or bad. To get our minds right, we must *"meditate day and night"* and *"so become like trees firmly planted by streams of water..."* Jesus is the Living Water. United with Him we will yield much good fruit *"in its season... and not wither... whatever we do will prosper..."* **(Psalms 1:3 KJV)**

PRAYER

Father, I'm still learning to manage my responses to daily events. I want to "be trans-formed by the renewing of [my] mind." **(Romans 12:2 AMP)** *I want this for my readers, too. Today, reading in Catherine Marshall's book, My Personal Prayer Diary, I was led by the Holy Spirit to ask for what she calls "a Spiritual scrubbing... that every dirty place inside and out be cleansed in the blood of Jesus." For any of my readers who desire to have Spiritual scrubbing Lord, I hope they will pray, and ask to be cleansed in Jesus' Name. Amen.*

MEDITATE ON THESE PASSAGES

Psalms 18:25 (GNB) *"O Lord, You are faithful to those who are faithful to You; completely good to those who are perfect."*

II Timothy 2:15 (KJV) *"Be diligent to present yourself approved to God as a workman who does not need to be ashamed, accurately handling the word of truth."*

Psalms 138:8 (ASV) *"Jehovah will perfect that which concerneth me. Thy lovingkindness, O Jehovah, endureth forever. Forsake not the work of Thine own hands."*

Psalms 19:7 (GNB) *"The law of the Lord is perfect; it gives new strength. The commands of the Lord are trustworthy, giving wisdom to those who lack it."*

I Thessalonians 5:18 (AMP) *"Thank God in everything no matter what they circum-stances may be, be thankful and give thanks, for this is the will of God for you who are in Christ Jesus the Revealer and Mediator of that will."*

"Be obedient to God, and do not allow your lives to be shaped by those desires you had when you were still ignorant. Instead, be holy in all you do, just as God who called you is holy."
(I Peter 1:14-15 GNB)

Be Holy

◄ *Number 6* ►

The Scripture says, *"Be holy because I am holy."* **(I Peter 1:16 GNB)** Holy (without fault) means perfect. Through the power of the Holy Spirit we can be holy. We must continually allow the Holy Spirit to renew our minds to the Word.

Consider **(I Corinthians 2:14-16 NASB):** *"But a natural man does not accept the things of the Spirit of God, for they are foolishness to him; he cannot understand them, because they are spiritually appraised. But he who is spiritual appraises all things, yet he himself is appraised by no one. For who has known the mind of the Lord, that he will instruct Him? But we have the mind of Christ."*

Yes, God wants each born-again believer to have that same discernment as does His son, Jesus Christ. We are the temples of the Holy Spirit. My desire is to have Christ functionally-formed and living through each of us here on earth. Jesus Himself tells us to go and do the things He did. That is a big job. However, He also told us that He would make us able.

Consider this: *"For we who live are constantly being delivered over to death for Jesus' sake, that the life of Jesus also may be manifested in our mortal flesh."* **(II Corinthians 4:11 NASB)**

Do you desire this? I do. My mentor in prison ministry is still teaching me to think--- not as a prosecutor whose quest is to condemn, but as the Savior does, whose heart is to redeem. We must stop making excuses, taking the comfortable, convenient path of least resistance with little or no effort. That response often leads to failure.

Peter reminds us that when we pray, we call God "Father". The Scripture says: *"He judges all people by the same standard according to what each one has done... we are to spend the rest of our lives here on earth in reverence for Him... it was the costly sacrifice of Christ, like a lamb without defect or flaw... through Him we have believed in God, who raised Him from death and gave Him glory; and so our faith and hope are fixed on God... by our obedience to the truth we purify ourselves... and come to have a sincere love for other believers, and love one another earnestly with all our heart. For through the living, eternal Word of God... [we] have been born again as children of a parent who is immortal, not mortal... the Word of the Lord remains forever."* **(I Peter 1:19-25 NASB)**

This is the Good News that He wants us to proclaim! He wants us to "grow up and be saved..." **(I Peter 2:2 GNB)** Each believer is *"chosen by God as valuable. Come as living stones and let yourselves be used in building the spiritual temple, where you will serve as holy priests... But you are a chosen race, the King's priests, the holy nation, God's own people chosen to proclaim the wonderful acts of God. He called you out of darkness into His marvelous light."* **(I Peter 2:4-9 GNB)**

One of the important steps is your submission to the Words of Father God and the leading of the Holy Spirit. Our submission is to listen, meditate on His Word and then, obey. *"For the sake of the Lord, submit yourselves to (every) human authority: to the Emperor who is supreme authority and to governors who have been appointed by him [the Emperor] to punish evildoers and to praise those who do good... God wants you to silence the ignorant talk of foolish people by the good things you do! Live as free people; do not, however, use your freedom to cover up any evil, but live as God's slaves. Respect everyone, love other believers, honor God and respect the Emperor."* **(I Peter 2:15-17 AMP)**

Only with daily renewal of our minds -- developing Christ's mind in us -- can we duplicate His works and have the strength and courage to obey His Word.

My dear readers, please join me in praying.

PRAYER

Father God, I want the strength and courage of Christ Jesus in my life. Please send the Holy Spirit to help, lead, guide, and teach me Your truth. It is the truth that frees me from past, present and future fears. I ask this in Jesus' Name. Amen.

MEDITATE ON THESE PASSAGES

Psalms 19:7 (GNB) *"The law of the Lord is perfect; it gives new strength; the commands of the Lord are trustworthy, giving wisdom to those who lack it."*

Psalms 18:30 (GNB) *"This God – how perfect are His deeds! How dependable His words! He is like a shield for all who seek His protection."*

Psalms 18:25 (GNB) *"O Lord, You are faithful to those who are faithful to You; completely good to those who are perfect."*

Romans 12:2 (NKJV) *"And do not be conformed to this world, but be transformed by the renewing of your mind, so that you may prove what the will of God is that which is good and acceptable and perfect."*

■■■ ■ ■◄◆►■ ■ ■■■

"There is no fear in love; but perfect love casts out fear, because fear involves torment. But he who fears has not been made perfect in love. We love Him because He first loved us."
(I John 4:18-19 GNB)

The Revelation of His Perfect Love Drives Out Fear

◄ *Number 7* ►

God is not the author of terror. The devil -- the tormentor -- is the author of terror. The only 'fear' connected to God is that of reverence, awe. Fear and security cannot co-exist. We shall know the truth and the truth brings freedom. God doesn't want us to be afraid of Him but to receive His perfect love, abounding grace and acceptance.

Fear can strike through manipulating thoughts and evil imaginations. If fear is allowed to grip your heart, the pressure can become an obsession which causes debilitating anxiety. We must renew our minds by spending alone time in God's Word. We need to keep our focus on the Word and not on life's problems. We must choose to turn from dark thoughts and torments and allow the light of Jesus' Words to enter our situations.

God, Jesus and the Holy Spirit cannot lie; so choose to allow His light to break through Satan's darkness. Keep meditating on His Word.

- *"The Lord is my Helper; I will not be afraid."* **(Hebrews 13:6 GNB)**
- *"I will never leave you... or abandon you."* **(Hebrews 13:5 GNB)**

Thoughts of defeat and despair or flashbacks must be replaced with thoughts from the mind of Jesus. We do *"have the mind of Christ..."* **(I Corinthians 2:14-16 GNB)** *"Fix your thoughts on what is true, and honorable, and right and pure and lovely, and admirable. Think about things that are excellent and worthy of praise."* **(Philippians 4:8 NLT)**

Willpower alone will not blot out bad thoughts. We must replace the wrong thoughts and beliefs with God's truth. We must replace destructive, hateful and even angry thoughts by speaking the Word and thinking on a pleasant, happy activity like fun time with family or friends. We must pull away from too much hustle and bustle so we can simply meditate on God's promises.

Memorize and quote His Word. *"You will keep him in perfect peace, whose mind is stayed on You, because he trusts in You."* **(Isaiah 26:3 ESV)**

In the Name of Jesus, ask God and His Holy Spirit to keep you in perfect peace and lead and guide you so you don't rely on your own strength but the strength of Christ alone. When Christ died on the cross He returned and told the disciples that He would send the Holy Spirit to help us to do everything that He did and more. He also promised we could do it without fear: *"Peace I leave with you; My [perfect] peace I give to you; not as the world gives do I give to you. Do not let your heart be troubled, nor let it be afraid. [Let My perfect peace calm you in every circumstance and give you courage and strength for every challenge.]"* **(John 14:27 AMP)**

God's Word is sure and unshakable. Will you choose to receive and believe His grace and open your mind and heart to allow His Words to restore and make you whole?

- *"The Law of Moses appoints men who are imperfect to be high priests; But God's promise made with the vow, which came later than the Law, appoints the Son, who has been made perfect forever."* **(Hebrews 7:28 GNB)**

▪ *"This difference then, also makes Jesus the guarantee of a better covenant."* **(Hebrews 7:22 GNB)**

So, our Jesus now sits at the right side of our Father and He is ever – always -- interceding, *"pleading with God"* for us. **(Romans 8:34 NLT)** This far better hope – Jesus -- allows us to *"come near to God."* **(Hebrews 7:19 GNB)**

Today, be made whole and continue on this journey realizing you have been chosen to serve Him. By grace, you are the righteousness of Christ! He lives in each of us. His Holy Spirit is teaching, guiding and comforting us as we daily renew our minds to be like Christ, our Lord *"because God had decided on an even better plan for us. His purpose was that only in company with us..."* would anyone *"...be made perfect."* **(Hebrews 11:40 GNB)**

Join me in praying for your wholeness, your holiness, your perfection…

PRAYER

Father, I am building my attitude of faith and expectancy so that, if I ask anything according to your will, then, it will be done. Thank you for Your goodness and faithfulness to perfect me. I cannot make myself perfect, but because Jesus died to cleanse me from sin and left the Holy Spirit to do Your work in me, I know I am being perfected. I believe for bigger things, in Jesus' Name. Amen.

MEDITATE ON THESE PASSAGES

Hebrews 8:6 (GNB) *"But now, Jesus has been given priestly work which is superior to theirs, just as the covenant which He arranged between God and His people is a better one, because it is based on promises of better things."*

Hebrews 8:6 (Weymouth) *"...the ministry which Christ has obtained is all the nobler...in that He is at the same time the negotiator of a sublimer covenant...free from imperfection..."*

Hebrews 8:9-10 (GNB) *"...animal sacrifices presented to God cannot make the worshiper's heart perfect ... these are only outward rules which apply only until the time when God* *will establish the new order."*

Hebrews 10:1 (GNB) *"The Jewish Law is not a full and faithful model of real things … the same sacrifices are offered forever, year after year. How can the Law, then, by means of these sacrifices make perfect the people who come to God?"*

Romans 12:2 (AMP) *"And do not be conformed to this world... but be transformed (changed) [entire] by the renewal of your mind… [by its new ideals and attitude], so that you may prove [for yourselves] what is the good and acceptable and perfect will of God..."*

NOTES: _____

_____

_____

_____

_____

_____

_____

_____

_____

_____

_____

_____

_____

NOTES: _____

_____

_____

_____

_____

_____

_____

_____

_____

_____

_____

_____

_____

_____

_____

_____

_____

_____

_____

_____

_____

_____

DIRECTION: _____

_____
_____
_____
_____
_____
_____
_____
_____
_____

PROGRESS: _____

_____
_____
_____
_____
_____
_____
_____
_____
_____
_____

Matthew 25:35-36
35 For I was hungry and you gave me something to eat, I was thirsty and you gave me something to drink, I was a stranger and you invited me in,
36 I needed clothes and you clothed me, I was sick and you looked after me, I was in prison and you came to visit me.'

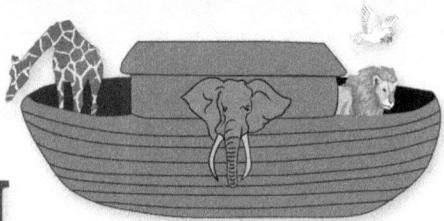

ARK of FAITH FOUNDATION, INC.

A refuge: Helping people help themselves by learning, sharing, giving.

CALL (918) 682-8411 MUSKOGEE, OKLAHOMA

In 1981 the Muskogee Carnegie Library Building, an historic landmark, was donated to The Ark of Faith Foundation. Today the restored building serves as our headquarters. No person is denied services or participation on the basis of race, color, national origin, religion, handicap, age, creed, belief, sex, or political affiliation.

The Ark of Faith serves as a refuge from the storms of life for people in Muskogee, Oklahoma, and the surrounding area. Since 1980, with God's guidance and in keeping with the Matthew 25 Scriptures, the Ark has held fast to its mission of helping those in need.

Find out more information about this ministry at

www.arkoffaith.org

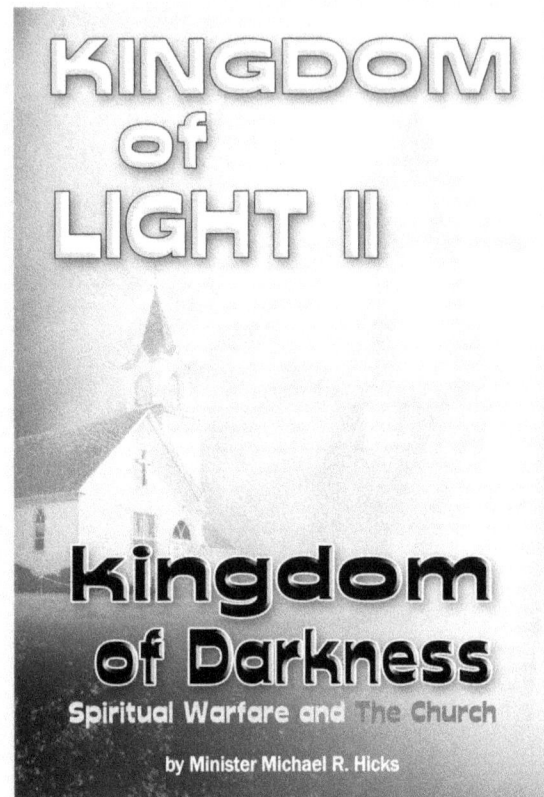

www.ingramcontent.com/pod-product-compliance
Lightning Source LLC
LaVergne TN
LVHW081316060426
835509LV00015B/1534